Knights of Love

fal

fal

Award-winning books from Cornwall

Dear Shadows	DM Thomas
Keeping House	Bill Mycock
Olga's Dreams	Victoria Field
Sleeping in the Rain	St Petrocs
Once in a Blue Moon	Angela Stoner
Seiriol and the Dragon	Michael Power
The Devil and the Floral Dance	DM Thomas
Many Waters	Victoria Field

www.falpublications.co.uk

Knights of Love

Jane Tozer

with illustrations by Apsley

fal

first edition 2007

copyright   text   Jane Tozer

                illustrations   Apsley

ISBN 10: 0-9544980-8-9
ISBN 13: 978-0-9544980-8-5

published by

Fal Publications
PO Box 74
Truro
TR1 1XS

www.falpublications.co.uk

Printed by

R. Booth Ltd
Antron Hill
Mabe, Cornwall

for
Tony Phillips-Smith (Apsley)
En vus est trestut mun confort

and for my parents
Stan & Laura Tozer

Acknowledgements

Thanks above all to Tony, the unfailing.

Heartfelt thanks to everyone in Falmouth Poetry Group, especially Dawyth Agar, Zeeba Ansari, Michael Bayley, Caroline Carver, Victoria Field, Eleanor Maxted, Les Merton, Andrew Robinson and Bob Rogers. I am forever indebted to FPG's co-founders, Penelope Shuttle and Peter Redgrove, a poet greatly loved and missed.

So many friends have encouraged me throughout this project. They include Rose Davis, Roderic Dunnett, Jane Middleton, Sue Rippon. The work has been enlivened by two inspiring mother/daughter partnerships: Sonia Florent & Josie Tetler, Maggie Vicuña & Hannah Tracey. Distant Muses are Michael in Cairo, Timo in Suomi, Swiss family Barta, and David in Porto. Friends at Marazion and St. Austell Quaker Meetings have been a source of strength.

Glyn S Burgess, translator, scholar and bibliographer of Marie de France, has been a good friend to this book, and to me. None of its eccentricities are his fault.

A big thank-you to Hugh Lupton, Eric Maddern and everyone at the Ty Newydd Storytelling Retreats. The generosity, charisma and spirit of storytellers are a constant source of inspiration.

Prizes

Extracts from *Knights of Love* won joint 2nd prize in the 2004 John Dryden Translation Competition, and 3rd prize in the 2005 *Times* / Stephen Spender Prize for Poetry in Translation.

Organisations

I am grateful to Arts Council England : South West for an Artist's Award enabling me to devote time and resources to research and complete *Knights of Love*.

The Arvon Foundation and the Taliesin Trust have granted me occasional bursaries to attend courses. I owe more than two decades of thanks to the tutors who have helped to kick-start the Muse.

Magazines and journals

Individual *lais* have previously appeared in the following publications: *Acumen*, *Poetry Cornwall* / *Bardhonyeth Kernow*, *Comparative Critical Studies*, the *Brindin Press website*.

INTRODUCTION

In the days before printed books, narrative and lyric poetry were primarily intended to be read aloud, either performed with music and entertainment at grand feasts, or on a more intimate scale at smaller gatherings of family and friends. The *Lais of Marie de France* were probably written for the latter, more private, occasions. Unlike epics, they relate love and adventure as they affect individuals rather than nations; their appeal is more intriguing than spectacular, more charming than heroic. But there's nothing sentimental or predictable about the *Lais*.

People who had access to libraries and manuscripts would find some quiet spot to pore over a book in solitude, but it was considered odd, even ill-mannered, to read silently in the company of others. Instead, they enjoyed reading aloud to one another.

My calling is poetic storytelling, and in my version of the *Lais of Marie de France*, I hope to recreate some of the spirit that would have captivated the original audiences and readers. In treating the *Lais* simply as a literary text, it is too easy to forget the magic and spontaneity of live performance.

This book is written for the enjoyment of the general reader, and the delight of any audience I can muster. It is not an academic translation.

WHO WAS SHE?

> *Me numerai pur remembrance*
> *Marie ai num, si sui de France*
> Here is my name for your remembrance :
> I'm called Marie, and I'm from France.
>
> Marie de France : Fables (my translation)

Some time in the late 12th century, an educated lady sat down to write. There's nothing very strange about that. But if I say "Marie sat down to write stories in verse", we have a mystery. Who was she? What did she write and why did she want to write it? How difficult was it for a mediaeval woman to exercise her talents and follow an artistic calling? Was she encouraged in her work, or did she write in secrecy?

We have the answer to this last question, because she boldly 'signed' each of the three books attributed to her, using her name *Marie* in statements of authorship and intention. She clearly wanted to be recognised for her achievement.

> ... Here is my name for your remembrance :
> I'm called Marie, and I'm from France.
> I fear some holy Joe or scrivener
> May steal my work and hold it prisoner,
> Then stake his claim to having written it.
> It shall not be. Marie's forbidden it!
> Only work that's badly done
> Is signed by someone called Anon. ...
>
> Epilogue: Fables (my translation)

All we know is her self-declared first name; the epithet "de France" was added by a scholar long after her death. Her family name, origin and the details of her life are a mystery. She is the first named woman poet in the French language, and her surviving works are dated approximately to the period 1160 –1210.

A woman of learning was, almost by definition, born into a family of high status, wealth and influence. There were a number of female scholars, minstrels and mystics in Europe at that time, but few (if any) are remembered primarily as poetic storytellers.

Writing of this quality takes discipline and long practice; Marie would surely have spent years reading, studying and perfecting her art. She had a flair for languages, and made skilful translations of Latin and English books into French verse. Indeed, according to the Prologue to the *Lais*, she actively sought out classic works to translate, which suggests her enjoyment and absorption in the task.

Marie's known works are in Old French. Scholars tell us that she used the Anglo-Norman form of the language, the kind of French spoken at the English court and by the Norman ascendancy in Britain, at the time of the Plantagenet kings. The *Lais* were probably heard at the court of Henry II and Eleanor of Aquitaine. A significant part of Marie's adult life was spent in Great Britain. She knew something of English geography as well as the language.

Marie says "I'm from France." From linguistic evidence and other clues in her writings, it's generally believed that Marie was born and raised in northern France, probably Normandy. There she would have had contact with the Breton *jongleurs* (strolling players) and their stories; she may well have known something of the Breton language. Three works with stylistic similarities are generally attributed to Marie, mainly because they bear her 'signature'. She wrote a book of *Fables*, and an account of visions seen by pilgrims to St. Patrick's Purgatory, at Lough Derg in Ireland. Nowadays her most famous and beloved work is this collection of short romances, the *Lais*.

Marie comes across as a fascinating person of intelligence, talent, tenacity, charm and wit. Hers is a creative and pleasurable vocation, not a didactic one. There's no finger-wagging in the *Lais*; any life-lessons to be learned are in the reader's own interpretation. Take from each story what you find and what you will. I'm certain Marie wrote poetry because she loved and enjoyed her calling, and knew her own worth. After eight centuries, she's still a pretty good rôle model.

THE LAIS OF MARIE DE FRANCE

> *... Des lais pensai k'oï aveie;*
> *Ne dutai pas, bien le saveie,*
> *Ke pur remambrance les firent*
> *Des aventures k'il oïrent*
> *Cil ki primes les comencierent*
> *E ki avant les enveierent.*

> ... So I began to muse and ponder
> About those lovely tales of wonders
> The lais I'd heard, and still remembered.
> I have no doubt, indeed I know
> That those old bards of long ago

2

Who made these rhymes and set them free
Were singing to posterity
For people they would never see.

Prologue : The Lais

What is a *lai*? Marie's usual formula says that the story began when the Bretons heard of a true and noble *aventure* (occurrence, series of events, happening). The jongleurs commemorated such *aventures* in words and music by composing a *lai*. These *lais* so affected her when she heard them that she was inspired to recount them in courtly verse. But she doesn't call her own poems *lais*.

This might seem like academic rigmarole, were it not for the fact that Marie was writing in the century when the vigorous oral tradition of the Celtic peoples began to influence courtly literature. Marie transcribed the *lais*. She, and writers like Chrétien de Troyes, made poetry which immortalised the *matière de Bretagne*, the matter of Britain. That is to say, the subject-matter of Great Britain and Brittany (Britain Minor) – the Grail legends, Arthur, Tristan. In Old French *Breton* could also mean Briton or British.

From antiquity, stories would have traversed the old trade and pilgrimage routes between Ireland, Scotland, Wales, Cornwall and thence, via Brittany, into Europe. Cornish tin, Irish and Welsh gold and hunting dogs were valuable commodities, traded for luxuries from the Mediterranean, like wine, olive oil, saffron, costly fabrics. Harbours became major administrative centres, attracting leaders, scholars, artists and entertainers. Tintagel was such a place; so was St. Michael's Mount.

There's no doubt that this process greatly enriched European art. Whether or not it debased Celtic culture is more disputable. The invasions and depredations of Romans, Vikings, Saxons and Normans fragmented Celtic society, often in brutal ways. This is a tragedy. But the ancient arts and culture still live, and the world would be poorer without them.

Cornwall's greatest contribution to legend is the love story of Tristan and Iseult. In the 12th century Arthur isn't associated with Tintagel. It is the seat of King Mark, Iseult's husband. Marie de France's Tristan poem (Lai XI : *Chevrefoil*) is a small masterpiece; a brief, beautiful episode which deserves more readers.

The cross-over from oral to written poetry made Arthur and Tristan more popularly accessible, no doubt with serious losses of substance, symbolism and meaning. But equally, the literary fashion saved some glorious stories from oblivion. I wonder how much of *Sir Gawain and the Green Knight* is Celtic, how much Anglo-Saxon, how much Norman in origin? What matters more is the creative genius of its anonymous author. Great art belongs to all humanity.

Marie's poems established a literary genre, the so-called "Breton lays", which became fashionable in Middle English. The English word "lay" for a short poetic narrative derives from the French *lai*. I don't use "lay" in this translation, because for me the word has twee Victorian associations : "Tirra-lirra, by the river / Sang Sir Lancelot." Besides, *lai* is a far more attractive word than *lay*.

From these literary texts, as well as from the more authentic traditional poetry and story, we derive our present-day perceptions of the Celtic world, in its beauty and grandeur, as well as in its Hollywood kitsch and sentimental tourist tat.

ABOUT THIS TRANSLATION
L'exactitude n'est pas la verité : Henri Matisse

What comes first – fidelity to the wording, to the formal structure, or to the tone and spirit of the work? Mediaeval narrative verse poses yet more questions. How do I keep the momentum of the story? How were such poems read or performed? How much can the modern reader be expected to know? What about a sense of period? No *faux*-mediaevalisms, please! Poet-translators have to decide.

Literal fidelity or poetic licence?

Strict accuracy impairs the poetry. In my translations, voice and story take priority. Surely Marie would wish us to take simple pleasure in her work. If a narrative poem fails to create that "What happens next?" feeling, it has failed.

There have been gallant attempts to make literal verse, or doggerel, translations of Marie de France. In my view they are doomed to failure. What's the point of exactitude, if the translator has to distort syntax or botch the rhythm simply to arrive at some dull, predictable rhyme? Since we know that mediaeval poetry was created to be read aloud, the acid test of a translation is that it should speak fluently and musically in performance. And at the very least, it should make the reader want to keep turning the pages.

1986 saw the publication of the first definitive prose version in English : *The Lais of Marie de France*, translated by Glyn S. Burgess & Keith Busby (Penguin Classics). This book freed poets of any obligation to literalism. At last I could make my own intuitive forays into the text, without feeling guilty that some hapless student might be misled. It's been a delight to do.

Storytelling

These stories were once performed or told unscripted. Having spent time with professional storytellers, I've learned the tradition that each teller adds something individual to the tale, and every re-telling makes the story new. This is just what Marie says – she didn't transcribe the *lais* verbatim, but re-made them in her own style. She is a constant presence in the background of her tales, occasionally even popping up to interject.

If part of a story is going down well with the audience, any self-respecting teller will improvise, make drama or a running gag of it. No doubt the jongleurs pointed up satirical references now lost to us, and exaggerated resemblances to persons living or dead. In default of a 12th century sense of humour, I add large chunks of myself. These imported japes should be apparent to the alert reader.

In Lai V: *Lanval* the hero is commended for his generosity to the jongleurs:

> Lanval gave with open hand
> Lanval freed captives from their bonds
> Lanval clothed rogues and vagabonds
> Lanval became the jongleurs' friend.

Marie doesn't have to say this, yet she does. Jongleurs occupied a low position on the social scale, but she pays due respect to them. I find this moving. They must have made a huge impression on her.

Irony

Marie de France is subtle and rarely hammers a point home. She is the mistress of delicate, stiletto-sharp irony, but the point is aimed at a cultivated 12th century audience. It's easy to spot that when Marie harps on about a character's great wisdom, that person will prove to be a total blockhead. But when there's a debate between adulterous lovers, or the hero/ine has to make a crucial decision, then our response is more equivocal. In some *lais*, we're constantly wrong-footed – Who's the villain? Who's the victim? Sometimes surprise is the point of the story. Now and then I broaden the narrative to make the irony apparent to modern readers.

Often mediaeval tales have a 'moral', or some instructive purpose. Do such didactic messages work in a different society and after 800 years? The *Lais* have religious undertones, yet they never take a doctrinaire line about such matters as adultery or birth out of wedlock. Their ethos is that true love is neither superficial nor obsessive (*demesure*); the wise lover shows balance and moderation (*mesure*). Even so, the end isn't always happy.

Additional material

I've almost completely rewritten one *lai*, and changed the location in another. Here and there I've rounded out character traits, because mediaeval stock figures are not familiar to us nowadays. Major alterations are discussed in the Commentary at the end of the book.

Poetic form

Marie writes in octosyllabic rhymed couplets, a form allowing more concise elegance in French than it does in English. She sticks to the AABBCC rhyming pattern, a discipline which can be monotonous in modern English. If there are a number of rhymes appropriate to a particular passage, I let them run as long as they add movement and mood to the story. There are several rhyming fugues in this book.

To generalize, French verse usually counts syllables, whereas the English tradition is to count stresses. I use a three- or four-stress line; usually iambic tetrameters but with frequent variations. Many lines end with an extra syllable. This is a dactyl, a stressed syllable followed by two unstressed ones, the so-called 'weak' or 'feminine' ending.

Marie sometimes has a slight natural pause at the line-breaks, and sometimes the lines are end-stopped. I can't think of any moments when the lines run seamlessly together (enjambement). To modern ears, constantly end-stopped lines and couplets can be dull, and in a long poem, positively soporific. The Border Ballads are an exception; the end-stopped lines are composed to be sung to rhythmic music.

My translation of the *Lais* uses natural pauses and enjambement (run-on lines) from the beginning, partly for variety's sake, and partly because when I read the poems aloud, I want the language to sound natural.

> Whoever has a poet's voice
> And, by the grace of God, enjoys
> The gift of learning, holds in trust
> A precious treasure, which she must
> Not hide away, lest moths and rust
> Corrupt it and it turns to dust.

now read on ...

PROLOGUE

Whoever has a poet's voice
And, by the grace of God, enjoys
The gift of learning, holds in trust
A precious treasure, which she must
Not hide away, lest moths and rust
Corrupt it and it turns to dust.
Heaven has given you a voice
So sing your heart out, and rejoice.

Don't clip the fledgling artist's wings
Or quell the bird before it sings.
Don't hide behind false modesty
And simper "Oh, it's nothing, really.
A hobby for wet Wednesday mornings."
The chasm in your soul is yawning
One day, you'll fall. There'll be no warning.

Talent is glorious when it flourishes
And it's good word of mouth that nourishes
Each work of art of real merit.
When it comes out, and many hear it
The first spring buds begin to open;
Then, as its praise is widely spoken
In salon, hall and reading room
The lovely orchard's in full bloom.

I'm sure you know the Latin Grammar
Of Priscianus. How you clamour
To get your hands on his next tome
And cannot wait to get it home.
But, just in case, here's a reminder
Of what he said –
                        and it's a blinder:-

"If you are working on a treatise
Don't make your arguments too easy
But cloak them in obscurities.
Thus each succeeding generation

Will have rich food for contemplation
With hours of pettifogging toil
Perusing finer points of detail."
Travail and labour lead to learning.
Perhaps, in time, they will be earning
A footnote in the commentary –
The thinker's immortality
One little piece of history.

Each scholiast who annotates
Helps knowledge to accumulate;
So libraries expand and swell.
As ancient sages knew full well,
Every philosopher and writer
Grows wiser as his beard grows whiter.
The more he reads, the more he learns
Of cunning logic's twists and turns
And other intellectual wonders.
Thus he avoids mistakes and blunders –
As reasoning becomes more subtle
His arguments resist rebuttal.

To those who strive against their vices
I, from experience, advise those
Subject to besetting sin
To roll their sleeves up, and begin
Some weighty task of scholarship;
Then your resolve won't fail, or slip
Once more into your harmful ways.
This is the purpose of these lais
A course of study is the cure.
There are few sins you can't abjure
No matter what your soul's affliction
From chocolate to drug addiction
Pride, anger, envy, lechery
Sloth, avarice or gluttony.
Mine are regret, and accidie.
Reader, I won't admit to lust
Or give it up before I must.

So, sick at heart with writer's block
I went to the library to look
For some improving Latin book
That I might render in Old French.
How quickly were my spirits quenched!
Rows of translations – all by men.
Chances were slim I'd make my name
Trying to beat them at that game.
It's nothing but a pointless chore
To do work that's been done before.
No, every work of lasting quality
Has spirit and originality.

So I began to muse and ponder
About those lovely tales of wonders
The lais I'd heard, and still remembered.
I have no doubt, indeed I know
That those old bards of long ago
Who made these rhymes and set them free
Were singing to posterity
For people they would never see.
These strange adventures that they'd heard
Of love, war, magic, well deserved
To be recorded and preserved.
I have heard several in performance
And I still cherish their remembrance.
Your edification and delight
Have kept me working late at night
Till my eyes ached from feeble light.

Most noble king, it is in honour
Of your courtliness and valour,
Your learning, worthiness and courage;
For you, to whom all joy pays homage
Whose heart's a garden, where there flourish
All the graces that you cherish
And the virtues that you nourish;
For you I made this small collection
Of lais. With most minute attention
To rhyme, to metre, and to diction

I have remade them as verse fiction.
Now, king, my thoughtful heart decrees
That I should duly offer these
My twelve good lais. If it would please
You to receive them, I'd rejoice
Proud and exultant all my days.
Don't think I presume, in arrogance
To offer you a paltry present
This is the best that I can bring
To you, revered and honoured king.
And now, lord, hear my tales begin.

I GUIGEMAR : *The Lai of the Silver Hind*

A story's like a precious stone
The jeweller's work is just begun
What grief to see it badly done!
An artist who has earned the name
Should be accustomed to good fame;
But when there bursts upon the scene
A newcomer of high esteem
Then he or she will feel the bite
Of calumny and envious spite.

Attend, my lords, and hear Marie
Who speaks with some authority.
Marie, in truth, was born to write
She's at her desk both day and night.
Letting no bushel hide her light
She puts her soul, her mind, her heart
Into the service of her art.
She makes good practice of her gift
And her detractors get short shrift
A friendly-seeming cowardly breed
They bite the hand from which they feed.
If she's the butt of paltry wit
She pays but little heed to it
For to be carping and pejorative
Is every skulking cur's prerogative.
Even the meanest-minded minion
Has got a right to his opinion.

I have twelve noble tales to tell
The Bretons knew their virtues well
From their experience, in good faith
They wrote them down, and told the truth.
Their words are simple and direct
They earn attention and respect
They don't elaborate or ramble
And I'll be brief in my preamble.
These lais are beautiful, none better,

So in the spirit and the letter
I'll sing as sweetly as I know
Of far away and long ago.

Hoilas was King of Brittany
His lands were wide, his subjects many
Sometimes at peace, sometimes at war.
He had a Privy Counsellor
Oridial, seigneur of Léon,
With many famous battles won
A noble, wise and valiant baron
Who had a daughter, and a son.
Noguent was pretty as a star
Her brother's name was Guigemar.
Handsome? The Bretons' main attraction!
His mother loves him to distraction
He makes his father swell with pride.

Time came to leave his own fireside
To serve some other king and lord
And gain experience abroad.
So young, so brave, so full of promise
He made a great impression on us.
Such a wise head. He would go far.
Yes, everyone loved Guigemar.
Too soon there came the day and season
When he attained the age of reason.
Oh my, just see how he has grown
It's time for him to cope alone.
His father dubs him, gives our charmer
The best in battle horse and armour
Equips him with the finest war-gear
To send him on his knightly gap-year.
Guigemar makes gifts to all at court
Then rides out through the sally port.

To Flanders, Guigemar makes his way.
The country is in disarray
The theatre of war and strife –
A place to lead a warrior's life.

Not in Lorraine or Burgundy
In Anjou, or in Gascony
In any country, far or near
Was there a knight who was his peer.
A bonny lad in youthful vigour
He cut a splendid, dashing figure
Yet Guigemar had a single flaw –
He had no talent for l'amour
And showed no interest in love.
How fickle nature's hand can prove!

No noble girl beneath the sun
Not even the most pretty one
Would spurn his love if he should proffer it.
Oh, how they prayed that he would offer it!
They often made approaches to him
With Guigemar, there was nothing doing
Their ploys and flirting went straight through him.
To every sparkling eye, a frost;
All their coy stratagems were lost.
No ladies' man, it would appear
And everybody thought it queer.

Well, in the flower of his career,
Young Guigemar crosses the frontier
He's on his way to Brittany
Because he dearly longs to see
Oridial, his lord and father
His sister Noguent, and his mother.
He stayed with them a month, at least,
To rest, amuse himself, and feast
On the diversions of the court.
One day he longs for forest sport
Calls huntsmen, knights and whippers-in
"Tomorrow, let the chase begin!"

The men and hounds rise with the lark
And canter through the forest park.
How his heart lifts with every stride
There's nothing like a morning ride.

A royal stag is their first quarry
The hounds unleashed, the huntsmen hurry
To follow the excited pack;
Yet something holds young Guigemar back.

I cannot think what made him late
But I detect the hand of fate.
He follows on their "Tally ho!"
His squire beside him as they go
To hold his hunting knife and bow
His hunting arrows in their quiver
For Guigemar's hoping to deliver
A shot at the next buck or pricket.

Then suddenly, deep in a thicket
Concealed by brambles, briars and thorns
He sees a fallow doe and fawn.
Her hide gleams snow-white in the dawn
And on her head, two branched stag's-horns.
Strange portents, these, to say the least;
This creature is a fairy beast.
The hounds bay with a frenzied noise
The deer leaps up in wild surprise
He shoots her right between the eyes
And she collapses straight away.

The arrow makes a ricochet
Striking the man who let it fly
A grievous wound right through his thigh
Through flesh and saddle, with such force
The arrow tip stays in his horse.

Guigemar's so hurt he must dismount
To rest upon a grassy mound
Half-sitting, half-reclining, near
The body of the stricken deer.
She cries, with her last painful breath:

"Alas! I'm wounded near to death
The victim of Man's cruelty.
And you, the wretch who murdered me
I shall foretell your destiny:-

"Your wound shall have no remedy
Your pain and anguish none can calm
No healing herb, no magic charm
Nor leaf, nor root, nor soothing balm
No doctor can allay your harm
Or mend the damage to your thigh.
And furthermore I testify
That only she can bring you cure
Who for your love's sake can endure
More trials, more pain and more dolour
Than any maid has known before.

"And you will suffer, in like kind,
The pains of body, heart and mind.
I swear to you by heaven above us
You'll be a marvel to all lovers
Past and present and to come.
And now my fortune-telling's done
Begone, and let me die in peace."
She fades away among the trees.

Poor Guigemar's wound is deep and keen.
Alarmed by what he's heard and seen,
The strange foretellings of the hind,
He racks his brains. Where shall he find
The lady who will be his cure
Although he search the wide world for her?
He wants to live, of that he's sure.
Alas, his life has been too pure.
He knows full well no lady living
Has caused his heart to change its rhythm;
In all his years, no love's assailed him
How can a woman now avail him?
He calls his squire to his side –

"My friend, I bid you, quickly ride
And bring my comrades here to me
I must speak with them urgently."
He's off at once.
                    There, left alone
Guigemar begins to weep and moan.
He tears the hem from off his shirt
And uses it to bind his hurt.
To mount his horse is agony
But he must leave there speedily
Lest his companions foil his plans
To seek his cure in distant lands.

A green lane runs between the trees
To open country and the sea.
A high cliff tumbles to a bay
A secret harbour, tucked away,

Where a brave little ship is moored
In a snug berth and well secured.
Sir Guigemar can make out its sail
Is this a vessel he can hail?

What magic craft can this ship be?
That she's well-found, the knight can see.
Her hull is caulked outside and in
You can't detect a single seam;
It seems to be all of a piece
Made by some cunning artifice.
From stem to stern, keel to cross-tree
Her timbers are of ebony;
Her sail is made of fine silk stuffs
A joy to see each time she luffs.
A Caesar's ransom wouldn't buy her.

Young Guigemar is astonished by her
The vision makes him stop to muse.
She's not been in the shipping news
Nor he has heard one person speak
Of harbourage in this lost creek.
He takes the seaward way, of course
And painfully dismounts his horse.
He's sure there'll be some men on watch
To guard this most exquisite yacht.

Deserted.
        Nobody on board.
A bed that's worthy of a lord
Is set amidships. Rich and good
Its posts and rail are of rare wood
The finest cedar of Lebanon;
Just like the bed of Solomon,
Inlaid and chased with purest gold –
Such craftsmanship! – and, wealth untold,
With ivory as white as milk.

A cloth-of-gold of Tyrian silk
Is spread across to make the quilt.

The pillow is so soft and smooth
There are no troubles it can't soothe
Your problems simply drift away.
If you but lie there once, they say,
Your hair will never turn to grey.
As for the hangings and the rest
Their worth could never be assessed;
They're priceless, and the rarest yet
A Russian sable coverlet
Lined with the silk of Alexandria.
Up in the prow, two candelabra
Of solid gold, pure beyond measure
– The smaller one's a priceless treasure –
With beeswax candles all alight.

Guigemar's dumbfounded at the sight.
Exhausted by his throbbing wound
He lay upon the bed and swooned.
Then, rested, he gets up to leave
But finds – a thing he can't believe –
He's trapped aboard.
             How can this be?
The ship's already on the seas
Spanking along; a perfect breeze
Propels her at a rate of knots.
This puts our hero in a spot
No wonder the poor lad's distraught
The ship's shanghaied him.

              Guigemar's caught
And can't return to his home port.
His wound is hurting worse than ever.
"Well" he exclaims "It's now or never
I'll follow this adventure through!"
And so he prays
             "Help me, bon Dieu,
I'm in your hands. Bring me to shore
Where I can find my body's cure.
Keep me from death, I thee implore.
Amen."

He lies down on the bed
And from his troubles rests his head.
Sleep banishes all anxious thought.

The little vessel comes to port
By evening time. The kindly Fates
Bring Guigemar where his cure awaits;
A city in the ancient fashion
Chief town of an outlandish nation.
I don't know where, but I would guess
It's somewhere west of Lyonesse.

APSLEY

The lord who ruled this distant land
Was a decrepit feeble man
His wife was a young noblewoman
Wise, cultured, bountiful, attractive.
His jealousy was hyperactive.

Many an old man, bent and wizened,
Keeps his young lovely wife imprisoned
Lest he be coney-caught and cozened.
The miser-king spares no expense
To build his lady's prison fence.
Her price, eternal vigilance.
Though he can't serve her as she'd wish
No upstart youth eats from his dish.
This king is cripplingly jealous
And, in his meanness, over-zealous.
He's spent the best part of his wealth
To have his lady to himself.

She's locked up in the inmost keep
Whose sentinels can never sleep.
Around the garden of her hall
There is a high green marble wall
Having a single narrow entry
With, day and night, a watchful sentry.
The far side's bounded by the sea
There's no escape, but if needs be
He calls a boat in times of danger.
To man, she must remain a stranger.

In the walled close, there's a pavilion
His wife lives in this gorgeous prison,
There, like a rare caged bird, she dwells
In this most opulent of cells.
At the entrance, stands a chapel.
Her chamber walls display a mural
Its allegory has a moral.
Fresco, in gorgeous paint, portrays
Venus, or Love's Many Faces,

In all her splendours and caprices
Beauty, wantonness and graces;
Thus, by these images displays
How man may serve the goddess duly
And love whole-heartedly and truly.

There, on one wall, the goddess stands
With Ovid's book held in her hands
Love's Remedy, in which he teaches
How to escape from love, and preaches
Fancy-free life. This book she throws
Into the flames, and in her rage
She casts disciples of the sage
Into the darkness, well-berated,
Banished and excommunicated.
Thus fair Venus tells us, chillingly,
Those who serve Love must do so willingly.

This lady, worthy of all praise
Is there condemned to spend her days;
Her handmaid is the one companion
Allowed her by the stingy sovereign –
Her sister's daughter.
              This good niece
Is clever, well-born, strives to please;
With kind good humour she attends her
And with a loving heart, befriends her.
The girl is always asked to stay
Each time his lordship goes away.
She sees nobody else at all.
No-one could scale that fearful wall
Or leave the trap once they were in it.
Alas for this poor caged-up linnet.
The king would trust no worldly sinner
To carve his lady's meat at dinner
Just thinking of it makes him nervous.
He hires, to do a butler's service
A reverend father, white-haired, chaste
With nothing left below the waist;
He feels no sensual desire

And sings soprano in the choir.
He revels in the lice and dirt
Of his penitential shirt.
Austere, malodorous, not nice –
Just stand well clear, is my advice.
He keeps the tower's massive key
And sings the holy litany.

That very afternoon, the pair
Of ladies go to take the air
After their post-breakfast rest.
A good fresh breeze blows from the east
They're in the garden picking flowers
To while away the endless hours
In their pleasant little arbour.
They chance to look across the harbour:
Eastward, out at sea, they catch
Sight of a sail. A little yacht
Skimming through the waves. She rides
Buoyant on the springing tide
Making good way. She's drawing near
With no-one at the helm to steer.

The lady, nervous, turns to flee
What strange vessel can this be?
It's plain to see her ladyship
Is frightened by the little ship
Her face is flushed with wild surmise.
The girl, more capable and wise,
Displays more courage in her soul
And turns to comfort and console.
Then, putting on her outdoor coat
She hurries down to see the boat.
Never has any ship so pretty
Put in to harbour in this city.
There's not a living thing aboard
Except the silent sleeping lord
Who, pale and still, lies on the bed
So quiet that she thinks he's dead.
She stands to look, her head bowed low

Then runs to let her lady know –
"There's no-one on the ship" she said
"Except a knight. I think he's dead.
He looks so peaceful there, and pretty.
Oh, poor young man. It's such a pity!"
At this, the girl begins to mourn.

The lady comes into her own
"Now, come along, down to the river.
If he is dead, we'll fetch him hither
And bury him, God rest his soul;
We'll ask our priest to dig the hole
And say the rites over the corpse.
If he's alive, perhaps he'll talk.
He has a tale to tell, I'll venture
Of some mysterious adventure."
They hurry there as fast may be
The maiden following the lady.

She stands a long while by the bed
Observes the corpse with downcast head
Lamenting for the handsome knight
Snuffed out when youth was at its height
And golden future lay before him.
No wonder she feels pity for him.
She lays her palm upon his chest –
A strong heart beats in his warm breast!

At this the knight begins to stir
The first thing that he sees is her;
With salutations, he outpours
Delight at coming safe to shore.
The pensive lady, who is weeping
Graciously returns his greeting
And asks him how it comes to be
That he sailed here across the sea?
From which far distant foreign shore?
Has be been driven out by war?

"Lady, no strife has exiled me –

Something far more strange beguiled me.
Ask, and I'll tell all about it
Nor hide, nor leave one detail out.
It's true I come from Brittany
Away across the eastern sea;
At dawn, a-hunting I did go
And there I shot a snow-white doe.
The bolt recoiled and flew at me
It pierced my leg above the knee
Just here, right though the thigh, you see.
No salve can cure my agony.

"Just then, up spoke the stricken hind
Sadly complained, sorely repined,
Gave me a sharp piece of her mind
And spoke this curse:
                              I'll never find
A medicine for my grievous wound
Save by a lady's care.
                              My mind
Struggles to know where she'll be found.

"So, when I heard my bitter fate,
I left the woods and found this boat.
I climbed aboard her in my folly
And soon succumbed to melancholy.
The ship set sail, she gathered way
And I was spirited away
As if by an enchanter's charm.
I have no notion where I am.
Lady, be good. On me have pity!
What is the name of this fair city?
Advise me please. I cannot leave here
For I can neither sail nor steer her."

"Dear sir, I'll help. Be of good cheer
I'll tell you all you need to hear.
My husband is the governor
Of all the kingdom. He's the chief.
City and castle are his fief.

He is well born, and very wealthy
But he is old, and far from healthy.
His jealousy is mean and harsh
He walled me up within this castle –
There's only one way out and in.
Such cruelty's a grievous sin.
An old priest guards the postern well
God send his soul to burn in hell!

"But for my maid, I'm quite alone.
Chamber and chapel are my home
I am imprisoned night and day
And too afraid to run away;
Within these walls condemned to live
I'd never go without his leave.
If you would like to stay with me
Until you're fit to go to sea
Our house is your house, good sir knight.
To welcome you is our delight
And nurse you while you convalesce."

"I'm honoured, lady. Thank you. Yes. "
To leave the bed afflicts him badly
He has to lean upon the lady;
Up to the hall she walks beside him
Tenderly she helps and guides him.
Into the chamber he is led
And settled on the handmaid's bed
In a private curtained recess.
The women help him to undress.
With water in a golden bowl
They wash the wound to make him whole.
With a white linen cloth, they wipe
Away the blood-clots, drop by drop
Then tightly bind the lesion up
With loving tenderness and care.
When they are brought their evening fare
The serving girl saves him a portion;
He is provided well, thank fortune.

Cupid has pierced him with his dart.
New passions flood into his heart
Through the wound made by this sweet beauty
Till he forgets homeland and duty.
He feels no pain from his hurt thigh
Yet often heaves an anguished sigh.

The serving maiden is dismissed:
"Leave me, my dear, to take some rest."
Her duties done, she leaves – to find
Her lady smitten in like kind.
Her heart flames with the selfsame fire
As Guigemar burns with deep desire.

The knight lies on his lonely bed
Wakeful. His troubles fill his head.
He doesn't recognise these feelings
And yet he's certain that his healing
Will come from her, or not at all.
He turns around to face the wall.
Without her care, he's sure to die.

"What shall I do!" Another sigh.
"Alas, oh why does fortune curse me?
I'll throw myself upon her mercy.
Pray for compassion, kindness, pity
On a poor stranger in this city.
And if her answer's proud and haughty
In constant pain I'll pine, till I
Just crawl away and wait to die."

As Guigemar brooded and repined
A new thought came into his mind: -
Better to learn to be resigned
Bear all his trials and aggravations
With courage, fortitude and patience.
Sighing, he lies awake all night
Tormented by his hopeless plight
Keeps turning over in his heart
The sweet words and the healing art

The shining eyes, the tender lips
Of her most gracious ladyship.
Lovesickness has him in its grasp.
Between clenched teeth entreaties rasp
"Mercy!" they silently exclaim.
It is a battle to refrain
From calling out his true-love's name.

If he but knew she felt the same
Lay sleepless, longing for his love
I think his spirits would improve;
A gleam of hope and consolation
To guide him through this desolation
And bring some colour to his face.
May Venus look on him with grace!

He's sick with love, and can't forget her
But she can't boast, for she's no better.
Plagued by her heartache's anguished pangs
She too lies wakeful all night long.
You may say "Amor Vincit Omnia"
But in their case, it caused insomnia.
At dawn, she's up, and bleary-eyed
"I haven't slept a wink" she cried.
Her friend the maid, when she wakes up,
Is quick to spot that something's up.
Her mistress is behaving oddly.
She sees her anguish is not bodily
These are the classic outward symptoms
Of what we call True Lover's Syndrome.
Not difficult to guess the cause:
It is the wounded knight, of course.
The man they pledged themselves to cure –
Asleep in the little nook next door
He is the object of l'amour.
She sees too, why her lady yearned
To know if her love is returned.

The maid's not one to hang about
She's off that instant to find out.

The lady's gone to church to pray
So in she goes without delay
To sit by Guigemar's bed.   And he
Asks her: "Dear friend, where is your lady?
Where has she gone? It's barely dawn."
He says no more, but gives a groan.

Her tone is sweet and gently chiding
"Sir, do not keep your secret hidden!
You are in love, this I can see,
Please don't conceal it from my lady.
I think that she might be receptive –
It would not pay to be deceptive.
Your love will likely prove well-placed
She will accept it with good grace.
The man who wants to pay her court
Must keep her foremost in his thoughts;
Such love is fitting, right and noble.
You two will make a charming couple
You'll suit each other very well
You are a beau, and she, a belle."

"I am so lost in love, my dear
Such cruel pain, such constant fear
So deep that nothing else can aid me
Than the mercy of my lady.
Help me, advise me, my dear friend
Can this love come to some good end?"
The handmaid, in her sweet compassion
Comforts him in hopeful fashion
And promises co-operation.
She's a refined, good-natured lass.

The lady has returned from mass
Mindful of her injured guest
She wonders if he had good rest.
Her heart is trembling in her breast
She's so in love, and so afraid.
At this point, she's aware the maid
Is calling "Lady, please come in.

It's time to have a word with him."
She will have privacy and time
To tell him all her heart and mind;
At least they'd both know where they stood
Whether it be for ill or good.

They greet each other.   Both are shy.
His tongue is tied, his throat is dry
He falls quite silent, and daren't try
To take his lady by the hand
And say the tender things he planned
For fear that she'll misunderstand
This stranger from a distant land.
He fears that if he tells her all
She'll throw him out of hearth and hall.

But if you hide your hurt away
No-one can heal it, so they say.
Love is a wound within the heart
Which slowly tears the soul apart
A cruel jest on nature's part
That takes a lifetime to depart.

There are some men who roam the land
Breaking hearts on every hand.
For them, girls are like hunting trophies
Such men are foolish, cruel and oafish
They think seduction is a game.
That kind of love's not worth the name
These lechers turn it to a jest:
"Love never pierced a strong man's breast.
It's for the ninnies, and the birds."
Such are their boorish vulgar words.
He who finds his soul's true partner
Should love and serve her ever after.

Poor Guigemar's got it really bad
Without her solace, he'll run mad.
Love puts some courage in his heart
He has a secret to impart.

"Pray love me, heal me, sweetest lady,
My soul is racked in agony
If you're too proud to comfort me
My heart will break, and I will die.
Requite my pleading with your love;
Do not deny me, or reprove."

She gives a decorous, kindly smile
And answers in an airy style
As befits a well-bred woman:
"Sir, this avowal is most sudden!
My answer, you must wait to hear.
I'm not yet used to the idea."

"Lady, for God's sake, pity me.
Don't take my wooing bitterly
Or brush me off with coquetry.
She whose habit is to flirt
Keeps a man clinging to her skirt.
He begs for love for months and years;
She simpers coyly, turns deaf ears,
Toys with his feelings at her leisure
Till she's esteemed a virtuous treasure –
Expunged her past career of pleasure.

"A gentlewoman of true worth
With wisdom, honour and good birth,
Who finds a man she can admire
Won't drag his feelings through the mire.
No, she'll requite him love for love –
No-one need know, or disapprove.
If no-one hears, there'll be no gossip.
Let lovers joy in mutual worship
Pleasure, delight and benefit
Before sharp ears get wind of it.
We have no time to shilly-shally."

His words ring true. She does not dally
But yields, with grace, to his demands
Falling at once into his arms.

He gives the lady his first kiss
And from that moment lives in bliss.
They lie together, face to face,
Talk punctuated by embraces.
May consummation bring them joy –
It has for many a girl and boy!

* * *

Full eighteen months, Sir Guigemar stayed
There in the castle with his lady
Their life together was delectable
Only a churl would say disreputable.
But Fortune, ever vigilant
May spin her wheel at any moment
One's risen, and another's tumbled.
Alas, the loving pair are rumbled.

Early on one summer day
The two of them together lie.
Kissing his mouth, his face, his cheek
She says:
   "My handsome love, my sweet
There's a misgiving in my heart.
I fear we shall be wrenched apart.
Darling, we'll be found out, and I
Will lose you.
        Oh, if you should die
Then I shall lose all wish for life.
If you escape, you'll find a wife
A pretty new love as your mate
While I, forlorn and desolate
Forever mourn my lonely fate."

"Never think that, or say it of me
My lovely, precious, cherished lady.
May peace and joy leave me for ever
If I should find another lover!"

"Dear, to ensure I won't be hurt

31

I'll set a test. Pass me your shirt.
Here, in the hem, I'll make a knot;
Try to undo it – you cannot.
Where'er you are, no matter what
No woman's hand shall once untie it
Though many lovely girls may try it.
There is no wench so malapert
Can free you from this magic shirt.
I say let any smart cocotte
Who can unravel it by art
Or any girl who can undo you
Have you, my dear – she's welcome to you!"

Guigemar agrees with fervent vows.
The true-love's knot (I can't tell how)
Is tied with care and pulled so tight
That Guigemar is trussed up for life
Unless some maiden brings a knife.
He takes the shirt, on her assurance
That he may ask a like insurance
And bind her by an equal spell
To keep her faith, and keep it well.

A magic girdle, next the skin
Wound round her flanks, and pulled well in
Fastened by a cunning clasp
"Take any man into your grasp
Who finds a way to spring this hasp
With nothing but his skill and art.
Let him not break the lock apart."
They seal their bargain with a kiss.

That day the lady's premonition
Dramatically came to fruition.
A steward with a nasty mind
Is sent by the jealous lord to find
His lady. She must talk with him.
The door is locked, to his chagrin.
He finds the window and peeps in –
Two in flagrante delicto!

Hotfoot to milord to let him know.

The old man's heart's convulsed with woe
He's never known such grief and pain.
He calls three of his toughest men
The sergeants of his bodyguard
Armed, strongly built and iron hard.
They're sent off fast to smash the door
And inside they find Guigemar.

The horrid grasping little villain
In vicious fury shrieks out "Kill him!"
Our hero's up and on his toes.
Quite unafraid, he quickly goes
And fetches down the stout larch pole
Which drapes the hangings on the wall.
He lays about him with a will.
Someone shall pay with blows and bruises
He'll maim them all before he loses:
"Come on then! Try it!!"
                    Hear him bellow.

The old lord quavers: "You low fellow."
He fixes him with beady eyes
"To what do I owe this surprise?
Where are you from, and who are you??
And how the hell did you break through
My system of security???"

"My name is Guigemar!" cries he
"Hurt her, you swine, you'll answer me!"
He tells the lord how he left home
How destiny caused him to roam –
The stricken hind whose curse he fled
His thigh-wound that forever bled
The little ship that brought him thither
And how the lady fetched him hither:
"She saved my life, my lord. Forgive it."

The dotard pipes:

"I don't believe it!
But if there is one word of truth
Go find your ship by way of proof –
Then you may sail the seven seas
To sink and drown, sir, if you please.
If you survive, then more's the pity.
At once, sir knight, you'll quit my city!"

"Lord, I agree." Guigemar replied
"I'm fortune's child, come what betide."
The knight is frog-marched to the harbour.
There is his ship. He's led aboard her.

She seems to shimmer in the air
Almost as if she were not there
But conjured by imagination
Without the need of explanation.
Travel by magic intervention
Is more than literary convention.
All lovers traverse unknown seas
Propelled by a capricious breeze
Now fair, now stormy, now flat calm
They steer their vessel arm-in-arm
Sailing to happiness, or harm.
That is love's fear; that is love's charm.

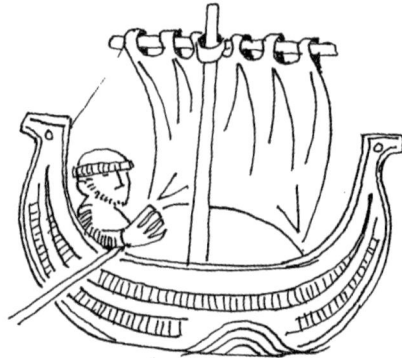

She's under way. Fast as may be,
Eastward she sails to Brittany.
Guigemar laments with tears and sighs,
Mourns for his love with streaming eyes
Beseeching God to let him die:
"Lord, may I never make landfall!
My lady was my all-in-all
Nothing to hope or wish to live for
If I may nevermore be with her."

While he grieves thus, the little boat
Heads eastwards to her secret port
The very place he went aboard.
Guigemar returns home from abroad
And sets foot on his native earth.

Nearby, on horseback, is a youth
Whom Guigemar knows. He trained him up
When the boy was a keen young pup.
Now squire to a knight, he leads
His lord's war-horse along the beach.
With great surprise, he calls the lad
Who, recognising him, is glad
To see Guigemar, and quits the saddle.
"Here, take my horse!" He'll not refuse.
The knight and squire together ride
Companionably, side by side.

It soon becomes the latest news.
The lost Guigemar has reappeared!
His many friends are overjoyed
Yet sad to see this fine young man
– Admired, respected, highly born –
So melancholy and withdrawn.
Surely a wife would bring him cheer?

Guigemar dismisses the idea.
He never in his earthly life
Can take a mistress or a wife

Save she who can untie the knot
In the long tails of his shirt
And leave the linen smooth and fair
Without a blemish, cut or tear.

All Brittany is in a whirl
Well, here's a challenge for a girl!
The knotty problem was assayed
By every lady and fair maid.
My, how their dainty fingers itch
To divest Guigemar stitch by stitch –
Without a knife! Aye, there's the hitch.

* * *

Time for us now to leave the knight
And to recall his lady's plight.
Advised by some sadistic baron
Milord has her locked up in prison
A dismal-hued strong marble tower.
She knows not one consoling hour;
Her days are bad, her nights are worse
Thanks to the deer's portentous curse.
In all the world there is not one
Who could describe her martyrdom
The pain, the misery, the dolour
Two years and more she's pent up there
And given up to bleak despair
Devoid of pleasure and delight
Lamenting her beloved knight.

"Guigemar, I loved you at first sight.
Oh, you were sent by cruel fate
And fortune never will relent.
I can no longer bear this torment
I'd sooner die at once than languish
Another day in bitter anguish.
If I could get away I'd flee
Down to the place you put to sea
And drown myself!"

At this, the poor
Distracted soul paces the floor
Then makes a mad dash to the door
Finds it unfastened, insecure
And yet she feels no sense of shock
– No sign of keys, no bar or lock
No one has shut the massive bolt.
Is the lord's garrison at fault?
There is no sentry at the gate
For yet again the hand of Fate
Melts all the barriers away
As she steps out into the day.

She's down to the jetty, where of course
The ship bobs like a rocking horse
Moored neatly and securely tied
Near where she threatened suicide.
She boards her. Then her heart's confounded
Suddenly sure her true-love's drowned.
Such is her wretchedness and woe
Her legs give way. She cannot go
Up to the taffrail and there throw
Herself into the chilly deep.

They sail off, till a castle keep,
A fortress handsome and imposing,
Is visible on the horizon.
It's Brittany. Is that surprising?
The seigneur of this citadel
Is Meriaduc, so they tell.
Below his walls, the vessel moored.
Early that morning, this great lord
Has his armed forces on parade
Heavily armed, strongly arrayed
To make a damaging dawn raid.
He's always feuding with his neighbour.

His window looks out to the harbour.
There's a strange vessel sailing in!
Downstairs, to call his chamberlain

Then off they rush, down to the dock
And climb the ladder to the deck.
Aboard, they find the loveliest woman
– More like a fairy than a human.
He grasps her by the cloak. They go
Up the hill to the château.

Nobody sees the distant sail.
With no more business in this tale
The ship I call the Silver Hind
Is leaving not a rack behind.
Where has she gone? I am quite sure
She's needed in another story.

He's thrilled by his exquisite prize
The cynosure of all men's eyes.
No matter why she put to sea
The lady's well-born, certainly,
He's sure of that. With that reflection
He turns the full force of affection
More love than he's ever shown before
On the strange beauty come ashore
A worthy lady to adore.

The seigneur's sister's young and fair
He gives the lady to her care.
She takes her to her own apartments
Gives her fine clothing and adornments
Serves her with kindness and good grace –
Yet can't put smiles upon her face.

She's always pensive and dejected.
Meriaduc tries, and is rejected.
He often visits her, and pleas
For tender love on bended knees.
He loves her dearly, his fine lordship
Yet she'll have nothing of his courtship.
She shows the magic belt and catch.
Her heart will never find its match
Until some suitor can unlatch

The buckle without force or damage.
This puts the seigneur on the rampage:

"There's a fine knight, not far away,
Who's bound up in the selfsame way.
He cannot marry, woo or flirt
Because of his enchanted shirt.
In the right tail, there is a knot
So subtle that a maid cannot
Undo it without shears or knife.
But she who can, will be his wife.
And your hand tied it, I'll be bound!"

The lady sighed, and all but swooned.
He took her in a rough embrace
And with his knife he cut the lace
That tied her tunic down one side
In an attempt to give her air.
But underneath, her body's bare
Save for the girdle. So he tried
To force it open. But he failed.

Then the poor lady was assailed,
For every knight in all the land
Decided he would try his hand.
Despite continual abuses
Attempts to break the clasp were useless.
For a long time, her woe endured
She bore it all with fortitude,
Until the day came that the lord
Decreed a tournament. The feud
Against his neighbour would be settled.

All the brave knights were on their mettle.
Meriaduc called from near and far
All friends to aid him in this war;
Foremost of these is Guigemar.
His is a special invitation:

"As my good comrade, take your station

Beside me in this testing hour.
You'll gain what wealth is in my power.
I know, my friend, that you'll not fail me
While hordes of enemies assail me."

Guigemar arrives, arrayed and splendid,
By a hundred knights attended.
Of chivalry, they are the flower.
He's in fine lodgings in the tower
And waited on with great honour.
The gentlefolk all want to meet him
The lady of the house must greet him.

Meriaduc plans a great reception
(With baser plots in his conception).
Two courtiers go to tell his sister
Put on her finery, and insist her
Friend, whom milord so admired,
Should come to dinner, well attired.

The two are dressed in all their splendour
And hand in hand, enter together
The steward solemnly proclaims them
And then announces – Guigemar's name.
Our sad, pale beauty hears him calling.
The sister just keeps her from falling
As her legs tremble and give way
She would have fainted dead away
To crumple senseless on the floor
At the feet of her paramour.

The knight himself comes to address them
His feelings? No words could express them;
He sees her face, and stands there staring –
Her very aspect and her bearing!
He steps a little back, preparing
And thinking to himself:

              "Is she
My one desire? Can such things be?

My faith, my hope, my love, ma belle
My heartbeat and my very soul
Who is to me my all-in-all.
All this long while, my mind has sought her.
How did she come here, and who brought her?
It can't be true. I have gone crazy!
This is some other well-dressed lady
They all look much alike at court.
It was some foolish trick of thought.

"Her splendour simply dazed my eyes
That's why I breathe so fast and sigh
And my heart palpitates and trembles
For love of her whom she resembles.
I'm eager to have words with her."
He takes her hand and kisses her
Says nothing more, but merely this
"Madame, please come and sit with me."
He sits beside her silently.

Meriaduc watches keenly
Troubled by what he thinks he's seen.
He calls Guigemar with a light laugh
"Sir, I've an idea on your behalf;
If it should please you, for a jest
Ask that young girl to take the test
See if she can untie that knot.
I'll wager you that she cannot."

The knight replies "I'll take your bet!"
He sends his valet up to fetch
The shirt from Guigemar's treasure chest
He runs back with it fast enough.
(Poor Guigemar sometimes takes it off –
One on his back, one in the wash,
One for hard work and one for posh).

He gives his love the shirt to untie
She looks at it, but does not try.
Of course, she knows the knot's her own.

Her heart and courage overcome
She would untie it, if she durst
But cannot, for she fears the worst.
Meriaduc sees her plight
And sorrowfully urges
                    "Try it!
See if you can undo the knot."
When she hears his forceful tone
The lady, pale and woebegone
Takes up the knot –
                    and it's undone!
With her light hand, the magic shirt
Unfastens faster than a thought.

The scales fall from Sir Guigemar's eyes
Yet he's still stunned by the surprise
"Sweet lady, please, tell me the truth.
If you're my dearest love, the proof
Lies in the girdle round your loins.
Show me your body!" he enjoins
"For it was I who placed it there."
He runs his hands down her curved flanks
And there's the girdle, God be thanked!

"My darling, what kind providence
Has rescued you and brought you hence
Where I have found my heart's desire!"
The two hold hands, they weep, suspire.
She tells her pain of heart and mind
The prison where she was confined
How she escaped, only to find
The ship I call the Silver Hind
Which sailed with her, east over sea
From Lyonesse to Brittany.
How here she was lodged, and nobly treated
Save for the seigneur's oft repeated
Solicitations for her favours.
"Now I'm in bliss, my love, my saviour,
Take me from here, to live with you
And I can bid this place adieu!"

Guigemar leaps up. "My lords, I know
She is the one who long ago
I gave up as quite lost to me.
Lord Meriaduc, now hear me!
I claim this woman as my lady.
Now I request you, in your mercy,
Give her where she belongs to be
To be my wife, and live with me.
If you relinquish her, I'll serve

Two years or three, and never swerve,
As liegeman with my hundred knights.
My lord, grant us our lovers' rights."

Meriaduc made this stern reply
"Guigemar, my friend, think not that I
Am so beleaguered as to cry
For help from such an upstart knight
To help me out in any fight.
I'd have to be in mortal plight!
I found the lady, I befriended her
When her privations might have ended her.
Now, against you, I shall defend her!"

Guigemar throws down the gauntlet, then
Quits the court with his hundred men.
It hurts him sore in heart and mind
To leave his lady love behind.
His heart could break from grief and pity.
Every knight lodged in the city
To take part in the tournament
Follows Guigemar, and turns his coat.
Yes, each knight swears his firm allegiance
To serve his term in Guigemar's legions
On pain of the most deep disgrace.

That night his army's at the gates
Of a great castle, the abode
Of Meriaduc's rival lord.
He greets them all with joy and glee
And offers hospitality.
He's overjoyed by Guigemar's favour.
Soon the vendetta will be over.

The army rises with the dawn
The soldiers put their chainmail on
Down at the pickets, grooms and ostlers
Buckle the armour on the horses.
Hoofbeats clatter, armour clanks
Across the bridge of heavy planks;

Guigemar heads the mighty force
Of splendid men-at-arms and horse.

Meriaduc's keep resists attack
It's strong, and they are driven back
Before they can break down the gates.
Guigemar encamps around the walls
And will not quit until it falls.
More followers join Guigemar daily
Until the seige starves out the city.
The castle's captured, sacked and broken
And Meriaduc's life is taken.

Sir Guigemar may claim his lover.
Their bliss has come. Their trials are over.
From this adventure I've related
Sir Guigemar had the lai created:
His bard composed each lovely note
To be performed on harp and rote.

My lords, you ask about the air.
It was exquisite, passing fair
An ancient mode, wistful and clear
And yet – inaudible, I fear.
Its cadence, on the inward ear
Falls sweeter than any tune you hear.

II EQUITAN : *Bath-Knight*

Translator's Prologue

This Breton lai's a *fabliau*
Which, just in case you didn't know,
Is an old type of bawdy tale
Put in on purpose to regale
Those of a coarser disposition
And an inferior position
To the gentlefolk whose taste
Runs to the courtly, wise and chaste;
Or simply to jazz up the mood
By inserting something rude
When the tone gets too elevated
And your desire for fun's not sated.
A story where you get the gist
Even when completely pissed.

Minor adultery's permissible;
Madness and murder, inadmissible.
No heroes here, they're all nefarious,
The outcome's dirty and hilarious.
Someone gets killed, someone gets screwed
By means ingenious and lewd.

It may surprise us that Marie
Whose breeding is exemplary
Could write a tale of sex and violence
To gratify a drunken audience.
The notion's tricky to believe;
We think her dainty and naïve,
It seems incongruous to our eyes
That she should be so worldly-wise.

Marie de France composed a mélange.
This story hands me quite a challenge
To write a tale of mucky fiction
In the most elegant of diction.

So far, I've followed her original
But I've no talent for the virginal;
If anything, my aptitude
Is for the vulgar and the crude.
No reader now would have a fit
Or criticise my style of wit
If I should write: bum, willy, tits.

Most people like the dirty bits;
The text as it was written had none
So I decided I would add some.
This may cause strait-laced academics
To send me scholarly polemics
About the ethics of the re-write.
If you can better this, then try it!
And if my hate-mail comes in parcels
Then my reply is simply: arseholes.

EQUITAN - *the jongleur's version*

Stupid folk love recklessly
And put their lives in jeopardy;
The power of torrid love's so great
That reason bends beneath its weight.

My narrative concerns a king
Noble and wise in everything
Fearless and bold, as good knights are
In shining armour, blah-di-blah ...
Well, no. In truth this Equitan
Is a complete four-letter man –
Oh, how unlike our own dear Princes!
Such base behaviour he evinces;
He wallows in his ignominy
Quite as lascivious as Prinny.

Marie describes him as a king
But I believe he's no such thing;
We want a sovereign we can trust
Not one who burns with wicked lust.
No, no, this bastard (beg your pardon)
Is a sort of Baron Hard-on;
Outwardly he's mister nice guy,
But underneath he's cayenne spice guy
Rip-roaring red-hot chilli pepper.

A king can't be a social leper;
He's got away with it so long
Because he's powerful and strong.
No wonder no-one took a dagger
To this outrageous serial shagger.

I'm telling you this fellow's slick
With his right royal rhythm stick
A sexy, hunky bit of rough
To dive into a lady's muff.
A scholar of applied linguistics
He measures up, by my statistics –

That's if, like me, you like 'em young
Inventive, tireless and well-hung.
Most do, according to reports.
Perhaps you don't. It takes all sorts.

Yes, Equitan has got it made
And has no problems getting laid
He struts his stuff and blows his trumpet
Chats up each widow, virgin, strumpet,
He'll roger it, then quickly dump it;
His technique's truly a fine art.

No-one believed he had a heart
Till it was pierced by Cupid's dart.
Oh, naughty, naughty little Cupid!
He's got it bad, and acting stupid
Just like some tottie-chasing Rupert
Scoring at a drunk hunt ball.
– Oh, no. I don't like him at all.
He lacks the sense that he was born with
Not who I'd choose to greet the dawn with.

He fell in love, head over heels.
Hooray! Now he knows how it feels
To dote, regardless of all caution,
Losing perspective and proportion.
It happened when he left the court
For a weekend of river sport
Not tickling trout, but hunting otter
 – You see! I told you he's a rotter.

He took his lodgings in the hall
Of his most loyal seneschal.
This decent fellow, right hand man
To naughty, knavish Equitan,
Has a good wife, whose lavish charms
Are praised by every man-at-arms.
Her loving spouse could not be prouder
For mother nature has endowed her
With brains and wit, bright sparkling eyes,

And curves her robes cannot disguise.
King Equitan is struck at once
By her delightful countenance,
A charming dimple that endears him.
Oh, how her conversation cheers him
He likes her attitude to life –
But she's his trusted agent's wife.

That night, all hope of sleep was lost
He tossed and turned and turned and tossed
While in his mind, King Equitan
Tried to devise a masterplan
And lay awake all night, contriving
A bit of surreptitious swiving.
His resolution almost buckled
As he prepared his scheme to cuckold
The serviceable seneschal.

"Not even I have got the gall!
He's a good man, trustworthy too.
Do as you would have done to you.
I see no clear way out of this mess
She's married to my man of business
Who handles all my state affairs.

(pause)

I'm not averse to equal shares –
Maybe he'll come to some arrangement"
And so, love leads him to derangement.

"It may well suit my darling's pride
To take a lover on the side –
At court, these days, it is the fashion
For ladies to indulge their passion
Allow themselves to be adored
By someone other than their lord.
No knight of honour hums and havers
When ladies offer him their favours.
Who dares wins. Fortune favours triers.
I'll ask my love what she desires
When I have told her how things stand.

Tomorrow, I'll take things in hand ..."

Next morning, early, old git-features
Is off to hunt cute furry creatures.
Telling the groom his belly heaves
He makes excuses soon, and leaves
He'll go to bed, and take it easy –
The best thing, when one's feeling queasy.
And so he rides back to the hall,
At which the anxious seneschal
Sends up his good-wife, to enquire
What comforts lordship might require.

He fixes her with fevered eye
"Pray love me, lady, or I die!"
So they begin debate, amounting
To little more than cost-accounting.

"What can I say? I hardly know you.
My station is so far below you.
Oh sire, what troubles this will bring!
I expect better from my king,
But on your mind there's just one thing
The same as every other man!

"Now listen to me, Equitan.
Kings do it just because they can.
They have all the power and wealth
Take anything they like by stealth
And when they've had their hanky-panky
Without so much as – Madam, thank 'ee –
They're off and over the horizon.

"If I say no, it's not surprising.
Small wonder, prince, if I demur
You and your damned droit de seigneur!
You want for nothing in your life
And I – am just a poor housewife.
How long do you suppose you'll stay
If you once get your wicked way?

My husband's love brings me great solace
His home's more joyful than a palace
Better a kindly man, though humble,
Than give a faithless king a tumble.
Do you think I'll dance to your tune
Just because you've got a fortune?
I need some time to think about it.
Good may come of it, but I doubt it."

"Do I deserve this charming greeting?
Pray do not say such things, my sweeting!
I'm not so base. I had not dreamt
To treat you with such gross contempt.
The morals of the market place
Ill beseem my Royal Grace
I'd never stoop to trade or barter
Like a Companion of the Garter
Or some such sort of coarse canaille –
Such low ideas pass me by.

"A gentle, courtly lady's hand
Befits the greatest in the land.
A king would offer her his crown
If she owned nothing but her gown;
If she's betrayed, and left alone,
That king deserves to lose his throne.
Those who treat ladies' love like shit
Will soon become the biter bit.
I'm sorry if my words unnerve you
I am only here to serve you
I am the slave, and you the mistress
I fall before you, weak and listless,
See, I implore you on my knees..."

So before long, his anguished pleas
And oft repeated, firm insistence
Overcome her last resistance.
He thinks that he has found his soul-mate
And she, her rich ace-in-the-hole mate.
He's an accomplished bold deceiver
And she's a little eager beaver.
He gives her a good seeing-to
And asks "How was it, babe, for you?
You've not had it this good, I'm sure..."
(Where have I heard that line before?)
And when they've slaked their thirst for pleasure
They each exchange some little treasure
Trinket rings to seal their pact.

With utmost secrecy and tact
The affair prospered. It would seem
This was love's twenty-something dream.
When he wants her, or she may need him
He says the surgeon's come to bleed him –
For when his highness takes the cure
His servants lock the chamber door
And he's quite incommunicado.
Nobody has the sheer bravado
To interrupt the royal leech,
So privately, quite out of reach

The king can taste his juicy peach.

Meanwhile her husband is presiding
Over the court of pleas, deciding
With great wisdom, right from wrong,
From matins hour to evensong.
And all this time, their bond grew strong
The thing continued for so long
Confounding all her grim predictions.

As is the case with all such fictions
We must press on to our dénouement.
It seems the court is in a ferment.
The Privy Councillors demand
That Equitan should take the hand
Of some rich nubile young princess
And get some healthy sons to bless
His throne and nation with an heir.
His negligence is hard to bear,
For he won't have the thing discussed –
His mind runs on his secret lust.

His mistress hears what's being said.
Next time they share the royal bed
She starts to sob into the pillow:
"Your promises to me are hollow!
I'll lose you, pine away my life,
For you must take a chosen wife –
The daughter of a king, whose dower
Will multiply your wealth and power."

The king responds with tenderness
His very voice is a caress
He whispers sweet words in her ears
"My darling, put away your fears.
You are my one true love. Don't worry,
You are the only one I'll marry.
I swear I'll never take a wife –
Unless your husband lose his life
Then I will wed you on his death."

She starts to plot. Lady Macbeth
Did not intrigue more deviously.
And she reveals some previously
Hidden defects in her make-up,
While Equitan is quick to take up
His part in this most cruel collusion.
It ends in grisly wild confusion.

Just listen to her vile proposal
For her husband's swift disposal:
"Sire, it's the season for blood sport –
Take respite from affairs at court,
The onerous duties of the state
Meetings, diplomacy, debate –
Invite yourself to our estate.
Fresh air and riding will restore you
For all the kingly tasks before you.

"To add weight to this false proceeding,
Inform your staff that you need bleeding
To rid yourself of evil humours.
That should put a stop to rumours!
Then bid my husband take the cure, too;
I know for certain he'd adore to
It's the simple fellow's dream
To rise so high in your esteem
And know you love him with such feeling
That he can join you in this healing.
After your treatment, just make sure
You bath well, to complete the cure."

Thus the wife and Equitan
Resolve to carry out their plan
And, to begin the cunning stunt,
He joins the steward in the hunt;
Then afterwards sends for the surgeon
Bids him commence the royal purging.

Meanwhile, the lady starts to lug
The bath-tubs and hot water jug

Up several steep flights of stairs.
Meticulously, she prepares
A bath and towels by each divan,
One for the king, one for his man.

"Remember, darling, which tub's yours.
My old man's boring, and he snores –
How could he kindle my desire?
Now, while we wait, I'll stoke the fire.
He's never been a lot of use;
This time we'll really cook his goose.
Equitan, now here's the laugh –
It's boiling water in his bath!"

Alone, for half-an-hour at least,
They've time to make the two-backed beast.
The king twirls his moustache, and snickers
Soon he'll get inside her knickers –

(Or he would do so, if she wore them.
No-one had knickers then. Poor them!
Think of how every wind that blows
Would chill your little furbelows.
There were no mediæval drawers
For gentlewomen, nuns or whores;
The men, too, have no underwear;
They just hang loose, and debonair
And have whatever fun they care to,
Every sin that flesh is heir to –
I'd catalogue them, if I dared to.
I haven't tried them all
                    I'm scared to!)

Was ever stratagem more scurvy?
Their glee is positively pervy;
The king twirls his moustache, and chortles
Rumples her wimple, lifts her kirtles
And finds the place for which he rages
Without the intervening stages.
"Believe me, babe, foreplay's fantastic

Without the gussets and elastic!"
As they begin the merry dance
Only his breathing comes in pants;
Quick as a ferret up a drainpipe
He's at the horizontal hornpipe
Before his girlfriend can draw breath.
Who says this fate is worth than death?
Not me. They're at it just like knives
Having the best time of their lives.

The door swings open with a thump. He's
Caught them at the rumpy-pumpies!
This interruption briefly cowed her
And then her cries grow ever louder
"My husband! Hurry!! Take a powder!!!
The tub!!!!"
        One leap, and he's clam chowder,
Expiring with the kind of shrieks
That put you off your food for weeks.

There's no more coming the raw prawn –
This fellow with the mighty horn
Fit for a big part in hard porn
Is red as the day that he was born
And calling for his mummy, too.
See what bad women do to you!
One minute he's in utter bliss
The next his quenelles are poached fish.
Scalding's a horrid way to go
Even for such a so-and-so
For agony it nearly beats
Being dished up as hot pommes frites.
He's hoisted by his own petard.

The wicked lady takes it hard
His anguish throws her for a loop.
Now she is really in the soup
Her lord, to put her in her place,
Upends her in the bouillabaisse
And now these rosy, wrinkled sinners

Are only fit for sea-food dinners.

Vile conspirators, beware!
Your traps may catch you unawares.
Here's the end of this spine-chiller
So perish every would-be killer.
He cooks his wife, the vicious hag,
Convenience food – just boil the bag.
Her wicked paramour is pickled
And Serve Him Right for being dickled!
Sod hyphens! Dick-led!
           (Where's the rhyme?
Find one yourselves, I haven't time).

Good riddance to the whole damned boiling.
I've had enough. My throat needs oiling.
I hope this leaves you in the pink.
Evil to them who evil think.
Hey, tight-arse, you owe me a drink
And make it large, you useless ponce!
Now, come on, don't all rush at once
– That bit's not in Marie de France.
Hein! Yoni soit qui mal y pense.

III LE FRESNE : *The Maiden Ash*

I have a tale from long ago
About a foundling's trials and woe.
Love's travellers have far to go
And what the end is, who can know?
This tale I know as *Ash-tree Lai*
A story for a winter's day;
From Dol in Brittany, some say,
To me –
     not quite so far away.

In Wessex, once upon a time
Two lords, young fellows in their prime,
Had manors in proximity
To the fine town of Shaftesbury.
As neighbours, each respected each
Since both were knightly, brave and rich
And both had married high-born spouses
For increase of their noble houses.
The wife of one lord soon conceived
And he was mightily relieved
When, in due course, the birth went well.
He sent a messenger to tell
His close friend of his pride and joy:-

"Two babies born, and each – a boy!
Mother and infants all surviving
The lovely little lads are thriving.
May I request you, honoured neighbour,
To do me a most kindly favour
And be one child's baptismal father.
I'll christen that boy in your name
And may he bear it with good fame."

When the courier came to call
They were at dinner in the hall;
Above the salt, the lord presiding
His lady sitting close beside him.

The page knelt at the great high table,
Spoke up as well as he was able.
The lord gave thanks to God in joy
"A fine horse to the errand-boy!"

The lady gave a bitter smirk
Her nasty nature went to work;
Of offspring so far disappointed
Her nose is thoroughly disjointed.
Her rival's sure to put on airs
Now she has borne two lusty heirs.
So, envious of the attention,
She made a reckless intervention
Vituperative, cold and proud,
Right there in front of all the crowd
Of staff and servants, spoke out loud
Her words were hasty, rash and brazen:

"As God's my help, it is amazing
That our respectable good friend
Should think this news is fit to send
To such a man as my seigneur!
His words redound to his dishonour
They slur his, and his wife's, good name
And tell the company his shame.

"His lady's brought to bed of twins
I need not tell you what this means.
No woman living on this earth
Has given, or ever will give birth
To twin sons of a single father.
One begets one – and who the other?
Here's what's at the bottom of it:
Adultery brings double profit.
She cannot be an honest wife
For there are two men in her life."

His lordship looked at her askance
His gaze transfixed her like a lance.
"Wife, let it be! You are to blame

In uttering such words of shame.
You harm yourself, and you degrade me,
To speak ill of so good a lady
And make a vile imputation
Against her spotless reputation."

Those present thought her jest was sick
And cruel, for surely mud will stick.
Each person who had overheard
Mulled over every spiteful word.
It was a wicked thing to say –
No testing, then, for DNA.
All Blackmore Vale soon knew, for rumours
Spread there like malignant tumours;
To every woman, poor or great
She was the object of much hate.
Why slander such a well-liked neighbour
Who'd just endured a double labour?
Her malice brought her grief ere long –
Oh, yes, she should have held her tongue.

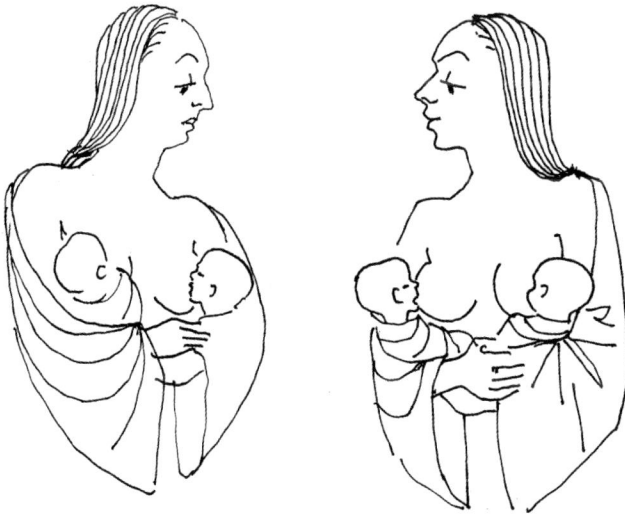

The page, back at his master's court,
Gave his seigneur a full report
Word for word of this sad history.

Childbirth is a women's mystery
And one which men cannot conceive.
Not knowing whom he should believe
The lord, in melancholy humour,
Was taken in by the false rumour
And racked by pangs of deep suspicion
Caused by an old wives' superstition.
Was his good wife possessed by lust?
Consumed by hatred and mistrust
He had her guarded, cruelly served.
These sufferings were undeserved;
Her faith to him had never swerved.

So unforgiving time rolls on.
The lady with the nasty tongue
Herself falls pregnant before long.
She's vast. You've guessed it! Twins are indicated.
Thus is her good neighbour vindicated.
Nine months are up. The time is come.
Midwives and wenches all struck dumb –
Two babies born, and each – a girl!
Yes, ladies, virtue is a pearl.
A female child's a crying shame
For who will bear his lordship's name?
Mother and infants all surviving
The wretched little brats are thriving.

Her malice has come back to haunt her.
How the neighbourhood will taunt her!
She's half out of her mind with trouble
The more she frets, her fears redouble;
In solitude she tears her hair
And vents her feelings of despair.
Here's what her folly brought her to:

"Ay me!" she cries, "What shall I do?
Oh out alack and welladay
There's nothing I can do or say.
I am disgraced, and that's for sure.
I've lost the trust of my seigneur –

He won't believe me any more.
His family will freeze me out
Once this hot gossip gets about.

"I brought my fate down on my head
By all those dreadful things I said;
I'm my own judge and prosecution
And shame shall be my execution.
A mother's bliss – and I begrudged her.
Who hasn't heard my rush to judge her?

"*Everyone knows when twins arrive
The prudent man looks to his wife.
However innocent her face
She has been up to some disgrace –
There are two fathers in the case
And it was ever thus, forsooth!*

"I promulgated such untruth.
She who tells a cruel lie
Must look her conscience in the eye
For Nemesis comes by and by
And binds her up in shameful fetters.
Those I have slandered are my betters –
Where calumny and spite abound
The victim's on high moral ground.

"Now I have given birth to two
I've bitten more than I can chew.
I cannot bear the shame. I'd rather
Put faith in our heavenly Father
And face the merciful Almighty
Than let my sinful folly blight me.
Man's vengeance is a nasty business.
God is the expert in forgiveness.

"There's only one way I can hide,
And that is by infanticide –
So, to protect me from ill-fame,
One scapegoat child must bear my blame."

Her ladies of the private chamber
Calm the dire troubles that inflame her
And tip the balance of her mind.
Their ministration's wise and kind;
They tell her gently, lest she harms
Her innocent sweet babe-in-arms,
They never could be reconciled
To killing such a tender child.
Though she's unhinged, to slay a daughter
Is still a grievous crime – manslaughter.

She has a maid of noble birth,
A confidante of sterling worth,
Her nurse who's loved her since her youth.
Her care, above all things on earth,
Was to instil respect for truth
And all the articles of faith.
She may be socially inferior
But morally, she's the superior.
She sees her lady's wild hysteria
The way she weeps and cries in vain.
To hear her ladyship complain
Breaks her kind loving heart in twain.
How her predicament confounds her.
Dear nanny puts her arms around her:

"My precious poppet. There, there, there!
These silly tantrums get you nowhere
Now dry your tears and hush, my dear.
Don't weep the place down! He will hear
The pandemonium and hoohah
Coming from his lady's boudoir.
Nursie can save you from your plight!
Give me charge of one little mite
For once that child is out of sight
And out of mind, then all comes right.

"I'll wrap her up snug, warm and sound
And leave her safe in hallowed ground –

Some church or abbey. I'll be bound
It won't be long before she's found
By some good, kind, God-fearing man
Who'll care for her as best he can
And bring the girl up decently."

The lady's joy is plain to see.
She promises a rich reward
If nurse will act upon her word.
They swaddle up the little pet
In a fine linen cloth layette;
To keep her warm, she is so small,
Enfold her in a silken shawl.
A finer weave I've never seen
Fit for an oriental queen.

Oh, such a pretty sight she made
A precious bundle was the maid
Wrapped in a lustrous bright brocade
Daddy obtained by way of trade
(Or, perhaps, looted on crusade)
From far beyond Constantinople.
No-one could doubt that she is noble.
Tied to her arm, a silken string
Is threaded through a massive ring –
An ounce of gold! – and set therein
A ruby. Words inscribed all round.
This will ensure that when she's found
There'll be no terrible mistake, as
Riches indicate high status.

The nurse picks up the little baby
And smuggles her, as quiet as may be
Creeping like a small grey mouse
Out of the chamber, out of the house.
Later that day, at even-fall,
She left behind the city wall
And took the high road though the wood
Stepping out briskly as she could.

In the deep forest, dark and wild,
Go hurrying the nurse and child
Onward through the dismal waste
Near to exhaustion from their haste.

Picture old plump frightened nursie
Trotting along the narrow causeway.
Each time an owl calls *to-whoo*
She shakes as if she has the ague.
Concealed by trees, the wodwo prowls
The bear stalks and the she-wolf howls.
There in the wetlands to her right
Are wispy flickers of marsh-light
The fickle, chancy jack-a-lantern
Which glimmers cold and green as Saturn.

Far on the hill, as day is dawning,
Cocks start to crow to greet the morning.
Hounds bay, dogs give a cheerful bark
That seems to drive away the dark.
The nurse is much relieved to hear
These sounds come from a township near.
She makes her way towards the din
Finds the main gate, and walks right in.

High in the centre of the town
Stands a great abbey, rich, renowned
For its fine church and pleasant grounds.
I've heard that many nuns live there
In the abbess's good care.
She sees the cloister, walls and tower
She can be there in half an hour
And so makes up her mind to hasten
Through the busy streets of Shaston.
Stopping outside the abbey portal
She humbly kneels to God immortal
To make a solemn heartfelt prayer
For the little one's welfare:

"God, in thy name, I implore thee

Guard this dear child, as I adore thee.
Keep her from harm, from death and danger.
May she be found by some kind stranger."

When she has said the last "Amen"
The nurse looks round about again
And sees an ash-tree in its prime
Hung thick with leaves for summertime;
The four great boughs are strong and green –
As fine a tree as she has seen
Planted to cast a welcome shade.

Clasping the child again, the maid
Runs to the ash, and in its crown
She lays her precious burden down,
Then turns away, and leaves her there
Commending her to heaven's care.
She makes her way home to her hall
And tells the infant's mother all.

* * *

A male gate-keeper guards the key
For locking up the nunnery
His daily duty to unlatch
Admit the gentry to the church
So they may come to hear the mass.
That very night, it comes to pass,
When the abbey's still and dark
He wakes up well before the lark,
To light the lanterns in good time
And ring the chapel bell for Prime.
Then he unlocks.

He sees a flash
And takes it for a burglar's cache:
"Thur's zummat bright in thik wold ash.
They've stole antiques. This yur's their stash."
It's several feet above the ground
So, reaching up, he gropes around.

"God bless my zoul. What have Oi vound!
'Tis warrum, an' meakes a mewen zound.
Well, thank the Lord. A priddy dear.
Poor mite. Oi cassen leave 'un yur.
Come upzy-daizy. Diddumz den.
Who put 'ee out? Zum naasty men?
Whadever happen'd to thy mama –
Poor wench, 'tis sure zum wrong's been done 'er.
Much longer, thee'd uv been a goner.
Thee's zafe wi' me, my liddle son. Arr."

Child cruelty, the man won't stand for
He has just become a grandfer.
In the lodge, this kindly porter
Lives with his newly widowed daughter,
Her babe, unweaned, still in the cot.

"Wake, darter, make the vier hot
An' light the candles, vor Oi've got
A liddle beabe along wi' me.
Oi vound un in the gurt ash-tree.
Now, warrum un up, and bath un, too.
Thee's got good milk enough vor two."

She does just as her father said
The lamps are lit, the fire glows red.
Cosy and clean, the baby's fed
At the young woman's ample breast,
Then burped and settled down to rest
And everything is for the best.
She lullabies the sleepyhead
Tucked up in a makeshift bed.
"Rockabye baby in the ash-tree
You are as priddy as priddy can be.
When the bough breaks, the bundle will fall,
But you'll still be the priddiest baby of all."

Together by the fireside
The two sit mazed and mystified.

What shall they do? They must decide.
The daughter's seen the ring and shawl
And tells her dad about it all:

"The child do be a liddle maid
An' she be 'ansomly arrayed.
You zee thik zhawl? 'Tis called brocade.
Thik ring's pyur gold. 'Tis finely made.
She'm too grand vor the likes o' we
Oi cassen keep the babe wi' me.
It breaks my heart, but tidden right
Vor we t'have the liddle mite."

Next morning, while the abbess sat in
The chapel vestry after Matins,
Our kindly porter, dear old fellow,
Shy and anxious came to tell her
All about the little foundling
Saved by heaven's grace abounding.
She ordered that the child be fetched
Dressed as they found her, every stitch.
Greatly relieved, home went the porter,
Took up the babe, and quickly brought her
With her layette and everything –
Her linen clothes, silk shawl and ring –
To show her to the holy lady.

The abbess contemplates the baby.
In truth, to see her is to love her.
"Le Fresne, or Ashling, is her name
After the tree from whence she came.
I will stand as her foster mother
And make a wise, kind woman of her.
I'll tell the world that she's my niece."

The porter swears to hold his peace;
His daughter, too. Their oath is binding
Never to speak of this strange finding.
Did Ashling see them any more?
We are not told, but I am sure

She often visited the porter;
Played with her bosom friend, his daughter.

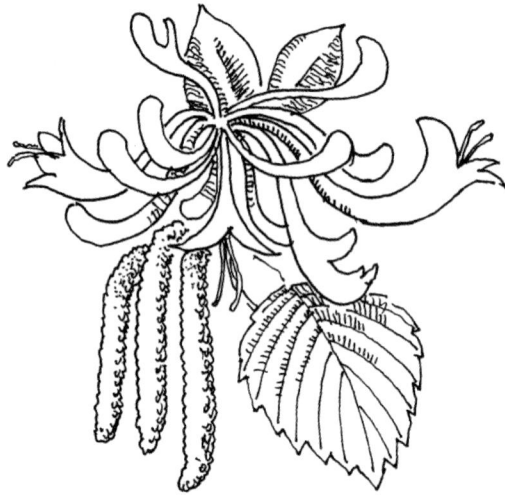

So for the abbess's young niece
Fleet-footed time runs on apace.
Within the abbey walls confined
Ashling is schooled in heart and mind
And grows up gentle, sweet and kind.
Until the adolescent years
When a girl's beauty first appears
Disarming, innocent; unplanned
Unless by Nature's shaping hand.
Now, on the cusp of womanhood
Le Fresne is lovely, wise and good,
Noble and courtly in her speech
Deportment only nuns can teach.
Eclipsing every Wessex maid
She leaves them standing in the shade.
She is indeed a girl apart
And captures each observer's heart.
No-one could see her and remain
Indifferent to our dear Le Fresne.

* * *

At Melbury lived a nobleman
A worthy knight, by name Gurun,
In all the breadth of Wessex land
There never was a finer man.
"If half of what folk say is proven
Ashling is a maid worth loving."
After a tournament one day
He comes home by the scenic way
Making a seven mile diversion –
"It's a nice day for an excursion
To see the abbey and demesne."

Once there, he asks to see Le Fresne.
Reverend mother is well pleased
Proud to show off her lovely niece.
Literate, sensible, polite
She captivates the gallant knight
Who sees, with great astonishment,
Such beauty and accomplishment.

He's caught off-stride. All unawares
Love has entrapped him in its snares.
This simple, artless nature's child
Bewitched him every time she smiled;
If he can't win the maiden's love
He'll think he's scorned by God above.
But if he shows undue persistence
He'll rouse the abbess's suspicions
And she'll forbid him ever again
To set eyes on the girl Le Fresne.

After much thought, Lord Gurun planned
To give the abbey wealth and land;
Thus he bought rights to lodgings there.
By parting with a load of cash
He gains access to Maiden Ash;
Such is his lordship's savoir-faire.
His object is his lady fair
– Not to remit his sins by prayer.

He visits every time he can
And often talks with dear Le Fresne.
His fervent vows kindle such fires
The girl consents to his desires–
The highest joy he can attain.
Now that her love for him is sure
He seeks to make it more secure:

"Ashling," he says "Hear and attend
Since you have made me your heart's friend,
Come live with me and be my love.
I'm sure, by God in Heaven above,
That if your aunt, the abbess, caught
Wind of the love we two have wrought,
The virtuous soul would be distraught
That you've transgressed all you've been taught.
Her temper, for the most part mild,
Would turn grief-stricken, wrathful, wild
If you should prove to be with child.
I am the older, dear, and wiser,
Let me now be your best advisor.
Your heart and soul, I know, agree
Come be my love and live with me.
I'll never fail you. This I vow.
All for your comfort I'll endow."

Loving him, the trustful maiden
Needs virtually no persuading.
Gurun and Ashling take the road
To his grand fortified abode.
She brings her silken shawl and ring–
Who knows what fortune they may bring?
They've been her lucky talisman
Ever since her life began.
Being perceptive and humane,
The abbess gave them to Le Fresne
Telling the girl the whole adventure –
Heaven's providence had sent her
And placed her in the great ash tree
With ring and silken finery

No other fortune, and no clue.
Where did she come from? No-one knew.
The abbess kept the child from want
By acting as her foster-aunt
Ashling would otherwise have perished.
The shawl and ring are her most cherished
Keepsakes, which she safely locks
Up in her private treasure-box.
Whatever else may slip her mind
Her precious things aren't left behind.

The knight with whom Le Fresne elopes
Amply fulfils our deepest hopes
He'll love and honour and adore her
Making the best provision for her.
His minions dance attendance on her
Not one of them but dotes upon her –
Not for her looks (though she's a stunner)
But her benevolent demeanour;
No queen on earth could be serener.
His men and squires, with boyish passion
Are willing slaves to bonny Ashling.

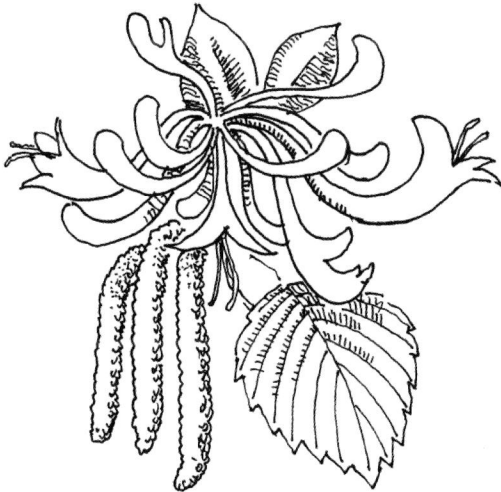

They stayed together a long while
And happy fortune seemed to smile –

Until the lords of nearby granges
Intervene, and fortune changes.
All his feudal knights, who love him,
Start to lecture and reprove him.
The advice of these noblemen:-

That he should pension off Le Fresne
(She, whom no man could disparage)
And seek an advantageous marriage
In hope that his new wife would bear
Their lord Gurun a son and heir.
They'd rejoice with him.   But despair
If he should chance to die intestate,
And leave no child to his estate
Then who would be their seigneur next?
This is their firmly held conviction –
New masters lead to mass eviction.

Should their concern leave you perplexed
They have a reason to be vexed.
Let me just put the thing in context:
– If Gurun has no child in wedlock
His followers are in a deadlock.
The estate passes in reversion
To some rich influential person
Whose followers and men-at-arms
Will require houses, lands and farms.
He will install his retinue
And Gurun's knights lose revenue
Kiss prospects and careers adieu.

They would be brought into distress
If, from attachment to his mistress,
He were to die without a son.
They will desert him, every one;
Never bear arms for him again
If, out of duty to Le Fresne,
He fails to act upon their pleas.
Hearing their case, the lord agrees:-
In prudence, he should find a bride.

74

Couriers comb the countryside
To find a likely candidate
To suit Lord Gurun as his mate.
"My liege, there is a gentleman in
An estate nearby; his standing's
Noble, equal to your own.
He has a daughter. She alone
Is heir to rolling lands and mansion.
You've often talked about expansion.
Unanimously, our committee
Considers that the girl is pretty –
Society resounds her fame.
La Codre, Hazel, is her name."

His friends cajole, browbeat and beg
When all else fails, they pull his leg:
"It's time for you to branch out, sir!
Ashling has blight. Get rid of her.
Hazel tastes sweet, when you go nutting
But from the Ash, you'll harvest nothing.
Every man Jack of us can see
You've set your heart on the wrong tree
And barking up it is in vain.
Your duty, sir, is very plain
– You must now supplant your Ashling
She bears neither fruit nor catkin;
Set, in her stead, a Hazel sapling
Who's fit to bear you many a nutkin.

"Uproot the barren Maiden Ash
And plant La Codre for her cash
She's the one to grace your orchard
– With a fine harvest you're rewarded!
Hazel, filbert, Kentish cob
That's the bush to do the job;
She has fine kernels, white and big.
In a nutshell (do you twig?)
You're lucky as a truffle-pig,

Get out your tool, and start to dig.
Go, stir your stumps, is our belief
No, no more puns – that's a re-leaf!

"When old Ashling's been dismissed
We'll have a wedding, and get pissed.
We'll make a proper overture
And offer what is due to her
With God's help, you'll be sure of her."

All parties readily agreed.
They soon arranged a marriage deed.
Alas, that they could not envision
The consequence of their decision.
Much woe and trouble lies therein.
Thus Ashling's testing time begins.

* * *

Le Fresne is hidden well away
From her true lover's fiancée.
Hearing a wedding will take place
She takes the news with calm and grace
No anger flicks across her face.
She serves her lord in deference;
With proper courtesy and reverence
Attends his retinue with honour.
The squires and knights look kindly on her.
Down to the youngest page they grieve
To know their lady must soon leave.

The wedding day – pennons, parades
Banners of Sir Gurun's brigades
Comrades-at-arms, his peers and aides.
My Lord Archbishop's visitation
Blesses the solemn celebration
As he leads in the lovely bride.

Her mother stays close by her side.
Anxiety runs through her mind

In deep distrust of womankind;
She knows too well that beaming smiles
Too often hide a female's wiles.
These artful sluts are all the same.
With this in mind, the haughty dame
In cold contempt and deep disdain
Plans to pull rank on poor Le Fresne.

She's wary of the famous belle
Whom Sir Gurun had loved so well.
From all she'd heard, the lady thought her
An enemy to her dear daughter;
Ashling, she's sure, will take the chance
To make a rift in this romance.
No doubt this spiteful jilted lover
Has jealous mean designs upon her.

"I'll throw her out of house and home
And tell my son-in-law: Disown
This woman! Find a husband for her
Some dull worthy who'll adore her.
He'll wed my daughter, come what may."

It was a glorious wedding day
With revelry and rich display.
Ashling is in the bridal chamber
And shows no misery or anger.
No-one who saw her ever knew
What the poor child was going through;
The heavy heart within her breast
The teeming passions she suppressed.

Hazel is her honoured guest.
She serves the blushing wife-to-be
Politely and attentively.
The gentlefolk are all astounded!
The lady's fear seems quite ill-founded.
So the bride's mother thinks again –
Perhaps she may have wronged Le Fresne
For hasty judgement's cold and hard.

Her fear starts turning to regard.

"If I had known the truth about her
I never would have cause to doubt her.
I would not, on my daughter's life,
Have given her as Gurun's wife
Forcing these true-loves apart
And breaking a sweet lady's heart."

Night falls. The hour comes to prepare
The bride-bed for the happy pair.
Ashling, weary, climbs the stair
Rolls up her sleeves, unclasps her cloak,
And summons all the chamber-folk.
She tells them everything she knows,
Exactly how the layout goes –
The furnishings, how to dispose
The drapes, the pillows and bed-clothes
Just as Sir Gurun would command.
She's often seen it at first hand.
The bed's made crisp and smooth and neat
With sheets tucked tightly at the feet.
How gracefully the hangings fall;
A coverlet thrown over all.

Le Fresne stands back to overlook
The serving-women's handiwork.
Something is wrong. The counterpane
Is faded, shabby, dull and plain –
A patchwork quilt of bits and pieces
From mantles, gowns, old robes and dresses.
When sorrow, grief and loss oppress us
And all our hope of love is lost
The tiny details vex us most.
It breaks her heart.

                    The very bed where
He will lie is drab and threadbare.
She takes her chatelaine, unlocks
Her special, private treasure-box.

There is her shawl. Its lustrous dyes
Are rich and pleasing to her eyes
The colours gloriously bright.
With her own hands, she turns to spread
Brocade across the marriage-bed;
Soft sumptuous folds of silk are right
To grace the joyful wedding-night.
Her generosity ensured
The pomp and honour of her lord.

My Lord Archbishop comes to bless
The couple in their happiness
Performs his sacred offices
And signs the bed with holy crosses.
The chamber doors are now thrown wide
To receive Gurun's lovely bride.

Her mother leads her, to prepare
The child for what awaits her there.
To help disrobe her is her duty.
Put off the finery. Her beauty
Candour, sweet simplicity
Are nobler than her gown could be
And the sweet radiance of her face
Outshines the cloth-of-gold and lace.
What earthly jewel could outdazzle
The shining eyes of pretty Hazel?

The mother sees the silk brocade
Upon the bed. She is dismayed.
"I've never seen a drape so fine
Except that eastern shawl of mine –
But that I lost the fateful day
When I sent my poor child away."

And at that thought, her courage fails,
The heart within her bosom quails.
She asks the chamberlain "My man
Upon your sacred honour, can
You tell me where that shawl came from?"

And he replies
        "My pleasure, ma'am.
It was the girl Le Fresne who spread
That lovely silk across the bed.
The old one didn't suit. The stuff
Was dingy, just not good enough.
I'm sure the fabric is her own."

Ashling is summoned and, when shown
Into the chamber, bows her head,
Takes off her mantle, curtsies duly.
 "Pray don't be shy, dear. Tell me truly
Where did you find this gorgeous silk?
I've never - once only – seen its like.
Where is it from? A present to you?
Tell me at once: who sent it to you?"

"It was my aunt" replied Le Fresne
"The abbess gave it to me, when
She told me how I came to be
Discovered in an old ash tree,
Wrapped in a shawl, with a gold ring.
Oh, yes, she told me everything:
I was a foundling – God be praised
Sent to the abbey to be raised."

"My dear girl, may I see this ring?"
"Yes, lady. It's a lovely thing."
The ring is sent for, and comes promptly.
The lady looks at it minutely.
It has a secret tale to tell –
Oh yes, Madame remembers well –
In detail it corroborates
The story that the shawl relates.
She can no longer doubt the Fates.
Le Fresne, so gentle and so mild
Is her own abandoned child.

This is no time for secrecy
She cries, for all to hear and see

"Mark my words, most gracious lady
– You are my child, my long-lost baby!"
Pity and guilt own no restraint.
The mother crumples in a faint;
When she comes round, asks urgently
"Quick, fetch my husband here to me!"

Thrown at his feet, she lies abased,
Leaps up to hold him in embrace
Rains tears and kisses on his face.
"Forgive me for my grave offence!"
What can she mean? It makes no sense.
Imagine the dear man's concern
What can have caused this funny turn?
No use. He can make nothing of it
And speculation brings no profit.

"My lady love, what do you mean?
Between us two there's always been
Nothing but joy and harmony.
Dear wife, you've brightened every day.
I will forgive you straight away
Whatever you may have to say."

"Your generous soul has pardoned me.
Now hear your wife's iniquity –
Once, in a fit of jealousy,
I spoke ill of our neighbour's wife
Poured shame upon her twin sons' life
And sowed the seeds of marriage strife.
Then I gave birth. You never knew
There was not one girl-child, but two.
I was distraught. That very day
We smuggled one sweet babe away
And left her at a nunnery
In the crown of an ancient tree.

"That's where they found the little thing
Wrapped in my shawl, with my gold ring –
Treasures you gave me as a token

When our first words of love were spoken.
These precious gifts are mine again!
Look, here they are.
                    I must speak plain.
Our daughter lives, and I have found her
Beauty, wisdom, grace surround her.
Indeed, she is the very girl
The well-beloved of the earl
To whom her sister is betrothed.
Now all the truth has been disclosed
The youthful sin I kept concealed
Which left a wound that never healed."

"Dear wife, let not your heart be troubled
Our joy is, at a stroke, redoubled!
We must not let this news distress us
For God has sent her here to bless us
And to prevent a worse disaster –
Lord Gurun might have wed her sister.
Le Fresne, my daughter, come to me!"
Ashling is stunned and overcome
Surprised by joy, she's struck quite dumb
By everything she's seen and heard.

He hurries off to give the word
In person to his son-in-law
And the archbishop, furthermore.
Gurun's delighted by the story:
"Now everything is hunky-dory!
Sing hallellujah!! Glory glory!!!"

The primate, who is just and wise
Gives them his very best advice:
"We'll let the matter rest tonight.
Tomorrow I'll put matters right
Dissolve your marriage to La Codre
Then everything will be in order
Legal annulment, not divorce."

They all decided on this course.

Next day, in church, a separation
Followed at once by reparation.
My lord's not long without a bride
– And who's the lady by his side
Presented by her loving father?
Ashling, of course! Ask me another.
Who glows with pride and joy? Her mother.
And Hazel, too, her new-found sister.

The three return to their estate.
Don't fret about La Codre's fate
– Soon afterwards, she married well.
There's little more that I can tell.
A rich man wed the Hazel daughter
And they lived happy ever after.

But when the tale was public knowledge
About this girl with brains and courage
And all the virtues that adorn her
Patience, forbearance, duty, honour
Beauty, courtesy, good fame,
They made this poem in her name.
The maker called it *Lai del Fresne*.
God bless us, every one.
                              Amen.

IV BISCLAVRET : *Sir Wolf*

Of all the tales I've memorised
This one is not to be despised –
I think it is my wildest yet.
No-one who's read it could forget
About the beast called Bisclavret.
As Garwalf he is known in French –
A name to make brave Normans blench.

Wherever mortal men are found
Wild changeling creatures still abound.
I want it clearly understood
The Were-wolf roams the English wood
And, I am told, it's not abnormal
To meet the Wolf-Who-Talks in Cornwall.
They make their dwelling in the trees
And roam at large just as they please
Prowling the forests in their rage
With wicked hungers to assuage.
Never walk by yourself at night
For human flesh is their delight.

In Brittany there lived an earl
Among his peers he was the pearl
Handsome, well set up and strong.
His rise to fame did not take long
High in his master's estimation
And in his neighbours' admiration.
His wife seemed gracious, sweet of visage
Well worthy of her privilege.
One thing weighed heavy in her heart;
Three days each week he would depart
On business he would not disclose
And where he went to, no-one knows.

One day her husband came home smiling
To find her at her most beguiling.
"Husband," she said "My love most dear

I have a question, but I fear
In asking it, I may offend
Against the honour of my friend.
Do not rebuff me. Keep your secret.
Tell me nothing you'll regret."

He caught her in a warm embrace
And gently kissed her worried face.
"Ask what you like. I'll answer true
There's nothing I'd not share with you."

"Thank God!" said she. "All will be mended
My foolish worries soon be ended.
It is the wish of every bride
To have her husband by her side,
And every time you go away
My heart is filled with deep dismay.
I'm weak and so engulfed in sorrow
I hate today and fear tomorrow.
I feel I'll die in desolation
Unless you give me consolation.
Tell me. My love for you is strong.
How could I ever do you wrong?"

"Lady, for pity's sake, don't ask me
For harm will come if you unmask me.
You'll cease to love me, and withdraw
And I'll be lost for evermore."

This speech she thought a manly jest
So once again she tried her best;
With blandishments she wheedled him
Her flattery so needled him
He told the tale as in a trance
Down to the smallest circumstance.

"Lady, I become the beast
Bisclavret, and I roam and feast
In thorns and thickets lurk and scurry
Ravenously stalk my quarry."

When the lady heard this speech
Again she started to beseech –
Did he go clothed or déshabillé?
"I run as naked as a baby."
"Heavens! Where do you hide your clothes?"

"That is a thing I can't disclose.
If by mischance my robes are taken
Or brigands find my den and break in
I'll stay a Were-wolf all my life
Estranged from home and loving wife.
Condemned to scavenge, loot and pillage
In hut and hovel, starveling village,
Loathed for my vile depredations
The butt of all men's execrations.
A fiend forever I'll remain
Till they are given back again.
Only my clothes can ransom me
And who'd behave so handsomely?
Such a bleak fate I can't endure
So I must keep my lair secure."

"My Lord!" was his dear wife's riposte:
"In all the world I love you most.
I've given you no cause for doubt
Yet now I feel like Love locked out.
What sin of mine can make you shun me?
Yet I'll forgive the wrong you've done me
If you will only trust me. Tell
Your secret. It will turn out well."

This was her golden opportunity.
Ground down by constant importunity
The broken man poured out his tale:
"I often take the forest trail
Hidden away from prying eyes.
It runs to where a ruin lies
An ancient chapel, dear to me
Which gives me blessed sanctuary –

86

Under the shattered crucifix.
Nearby an ancient stone is fixed
Concealed by bushes, briars and sticks.
There is a chamber dark and hollow
My den lies hidden down below."

When these words fell upon her ears
She turned quite scarlet, close to tears,
For now, in mortal fear of him,
She saw her future dark and grim.
How could a wife enjoy safe harbour
Wed to a creature so macabre?
She thought of nothing else all day
But planned and schemed to run away.

Not far away, there lived a knight.
She was the moon of his delight.
With prayers and gifts and declarations
For years he wooed her. In great patience
He sought to gain the lady's favour
With no reward for his behaviour.
She treated him with unconcern
And made no pledges in return.

Soon she devised a clever plan
Which would involve this ardent man;
So to the knight a note was written

Declaring that she, too, was smitten:-

"Dear heart, your hour of joy is here!
For long you've been my chevalier.
The joys for which you toil and pray
I'll grant forthwith, and not gainsay;
Body and soul I will surrender.
Make me your mistress, true and tender!"

He showed her all his deepest gratitude
His vows displayed a proper attitude,
While she, in turn, pledged him her troth
And then poured all her story forth.

In Marie's words she's quite laconic;
I hear her as more histrionic
As she describes her fear and loathing
Of this mild sheep in wolvish clothing.
She told the object of her lust
All the truth she held in trust,
Hysterically began to speak:

"Our married life is all too bleak –
Comparisons may be invidious,
But, next to you, my husband's hideous.
He's turned into a frightful freak
It chills my blood to hear him shriek
The recollection makes me weak!
His table manners are unique
He slavers like a thing demented.
I loved him once. Now I've repented.
I dread the man. In form and feature
He has become a loathsome creature."

Through the woods this couple rode
To where her husband had bestowed
His human clothing in a hoard;
Her pledge of secrecy – ignored.
They huddled by the holy ruin;
Treachery was surely brewing.

She planned it all.
               Oh, she was shrewd as
That most grievous traitor, Judas.
Her lord, who preyed on fellow men
Was never to be seen again.
His friends were of that firm opinion,
For though they searched his wild dominion
And quartered every inch of ground
No trace of him was ever found.
She waited till the time was right
Then moved in with her lovelorn knight.
Bisclavret, missing, presumed dead,
Had left the couple free to wed.

A year went past. The King rode through
With all his hounds and retinue
A-hunting, crying "View-halloo!"
Deep in the forest. And they drew
The covert which the Wolf called home.

The hounds, unleashed, were free to roam
And soon picked up Bisclavret's stink
Followed by men in hunting pink.
They chased the beast from dawn to night
And, though he was not caught outright,
They almost brought him to his knees.
He licked his wounds among the trees
For he was copiously bleeding.

In fear for life, he ran, conceding,
To beg for mercy from the King,
And then he did the strangest thing:
– He clutched the prince's stirrup leather
Kissed the King's foot, and altogether
Petrified his royal Highness
With silent pleas for loving-kindness.

"Come huntsmen!" cried the King, "And see
The homage that he pays to me!
As sentient as any human
He begs the mercy of the Breton.
Whips, stop the hounds! Regroup the pack,
And all you eager blades, draw back!
Do not incur our strong displeasure
By harming such a royal treasure;
It pleases us to show him grace
For he has got a kindly face.
Our royal pardon to the beast.
Call off the hunt. Now, to the feast!"

APSLEY

He turned and took the homeward ride
Bisclavret trotting by his side
As close as any sticking plaster;
Just like a good dog with his master
He followed safely to the palace.
This gentle creature without malice
Was charming, handsome, rather sweet
When they had cleaned him up a treat.

From St. Malo to St. Nazaire
All men shrugged *Zut!* and *Quelle affaire!*
No traveller's tale from east or tropic
Could ever yield so hot a topic.
He was the talk of Brest and Quimper
And took it all without a whimper.
No-one has seen a being like him
And woe betide the first to strike him
The cherished favourite of the crown;
Nothing but kindness must be shown
On pain of the King's severe displeasure.

The Wolf enjoys a life of leisure.
Though poor Bisclavret is quite dumb
He sets the household in a hum;
The courtiers grant his every wish –
The softest bed, a lordly dish.
Each lackey, liveryman and toff
Brings him nice tasty things to scoff
And claret in a silver trough.
The Were-wolf just can't get enough.
Pedigree Wolf? No, you can shove it.
Ah, Pyk in Galauntyne – I love it!
Dainty tit-bits make good eating
And he who hurts him, gets a beating.
They lavish gifts without economy
And he rewards them with his bonhomie.

He's living at the Were-wolf Ritz
Where everyone loves him to bits.
By day he plays with lords and squires

Then to the royal couch retires.
This Wolf, whose life was dearly bought
Became the pet of all at court.
He whose fortunes seemed irreparable
Friend of a king! They were inseparable
Boon companions all day long.
No-one recalled a love so strong.

One day the King decreed: "I call
All nobles to my hunting hall
And as a prelude to the sport
Come to a feast with all the court."
This was a banquet without equal
A royal repast.
                    – Now, mark the sequel.

The dining table is all set
And sitting there that wicked wretch
Who stole the wife of Bisclavret.
He brought a splendid retinue.
Who would he meet?

                    He little knew.
The Were-wolf smelled the man at once
And fell upon him with one pounce.
Knocking him over with his paws
To rend him in his fearsome jaws.
He would have torn him limb from limb
Had not his Highness threatened him,
Showed the big stick he used for thrashing.

Twice more that day, his teeth set gnashing.
The household marvelled. It was strange
To see this terrifying change.
The Wolf, so gentle all that while
Had never shown the slightest guile
This was the pet they brushed and stroked;
He'd not attack unless provoked.

The mystery, they argued, hinged

On some old wrong to be avenged.
They reasoned that the greater fault
Lay with the victim of assault.
That knight had a secret up his sleeve
And all too gladly took his leave;
The moment he was given congé
Back to his home he rode straightway.

Now, soon, his wise and noble Grace
Hunts in the woods again to trace
The very spot where he had found
The Wolf who follows like a hound.
Night fell. The royal hunt sought sojourn
In a nearby country mansion.
Bisclavret's widow hears about it
And dresses in a modish outfit
To seek an audience with the King:
She has a costly gift to bring.
Bisclavret sees her.

       Wild and savage
Ready to murder, maim and ravage
Crouches, as cats stake out a mousehole,
Then frees himself from leash and muzzle
Bites off her nose.
          I can't say schnozzle.
Oh yes I can!
         A wild schlemozzle
Followed this ghastly mutilation.
The lady faced humiliation.
Here's a right royal howdy-do
All jabbering in parley-voo
The minions beat him, try to catch him
Draw their sharp rapiers to dispatch him
And cut him up in tiny pieces.
His peril rapidly increases.

A voice of calm authority
Breaks through the mêlée:
        "Sire, hear me.

This beast is loyal. By your side
He's always been a faithful guide
Obedient as your own right arm.
He's not committed any harm
To man or woman, I declare,
Until he mauled –
                    this lady here!   *(pointing)*
Except for the time he tried to bite
That charming and well-spoken knight
Who was a courtier to your Grace
Before he quit his favoured place
(Desertion which we all deplored)
This knight he snarled at is – her lord!

"There's more to this than meets our eyes.
Question her harshly; try to prise
The secret from her –
                    for she knows
Just why the wolf bit off her nose.
How did she earn such vicious hate?
Here, in your Highness' fair estate
Of Brittany, strange tales are woven
And many miracles are proven."

The King hears what the sage attests;
Sends out a squadron; makes arrests.
The knight and lady are arraigned
Down in the dungeons they're detained.
By force of torture they soon pour
The story out to their seigneur.
All their treachery they disclose:
They robbed her husband of his clothes
He found the empty hiding-place
And loped off howling. Left no trace.
For ever since that wicked theft
No sign of Bisclavret was left.

Wolf and Bisclavret were the same!
The King saw through their evil game
He sent his servitors to fetch

The stolen garments, every stitch.
They showed the Wolf his rich array
But the poor creature shied away –
Though it was spread before his eyes
He could not bear his human guise.
Sage gave sovereign this advice:

"Sire, it was neither kind nor wise
To circle him with prying eyes.
The Wolf is modest, I surmise,
Shamed by this public proffering;
For it costs him pangs and suffering
To be reborn in human flesh
From so long in the wilderness.
Now lead him to your royal suite
And lay his clothing at his feet.
Leave him in peace and privacy
And we shall see what we shall see."

The King departs with Bisclavret
And locks the doors.
                    Then comes again
With two strong nobles in his train.
Into the chamber, one, two, three,
Go creeping softly, where they see
A sight they'll none of them forget –

Under the royal coverlet
There lies a knight, gentle as may be,
Sleeping as peaceful as a baby.

The King runs forward, warmly clasps him,
Weeping and kissing, firmly grasps him
By the hand. Swears restitution
Will be made. No contribution
To his friend's comfort will be spared;
His house and lands restored, repaired.

As for the wife, well, she was banished.
She and her paramour soon vanished

Exiled to a far country, where
The offspring of this treacherous pair
May still be seen, as one supposes,
And recognised.
                    They have *no noses!*
But only the girls. Can't you just hear
Their cries of "Why? It's so unfair!"
Each wears the mark of mother's sin
Between her eyebrows and her chin
Mama has strayed, and their disgrace is
To live their lives with strange blank faces.
It's hard to look sophisticated
When you've been denostricated.

Sensational stories must come out
This one is true, pray have no doubt.
For Bisclavret they wrote this lai
To last forever and a day.

V LANVAL : *The Lai of the Otherworld Lady*

I have another tale to tell
A true account of what befell
A fine young man, a nonpareil,
The Britons name him Sir Lanval.

At Kardoël, now called Carlisle,
Dwells good King Arthur, for a while
At war against the Scots and Picts
Famed for their cunning knavish tricks.
By fire and sword, their force inflicts
Grave damage on the countryside
With devastation far and wide.
On this particular occasion
They have succeeded in invasion
Of the motherland of Logres
And laid it waste, the scurvy rogues.

King Arthur was a bounteous host
And, at the feast of Pentecost,
Distributed the royal largesse
To every man of the noblesse –
Knights, lords and barons, famed in fable
Who gathered at the great Round Table.
The world, alas, will never see
Again such pomp and chivalry.

Propitious marriages were planned
With lavish gifts of wealth and land.
But, by unlucky oversight
The King forgot one faithful knight.
None of the courtiers proposed him
Many secretly opposed him
Seeking to impede his progress,
For they were jealous of his prowess
Generosity and grace
His goodness, charm and handsome face.

The object of their envious spite
Was young Lanval, a worthy knight,
Good-looking, noble, brave and gallant
Possessed of every courtly talent,
Who gave alms with an open hand
Though he lacked money, goods and land.

They seem to court his company
But, underneath, spread calumny.
They'd shed no tears at his comeuppance.
Feigned fellowship is not worth tuppence.

Son of a king of might and merit,
Yet far from the realm that he'll inherit,
While serving at King Arthur's court
He's run through all the gold he brought.
The King forgets to give him funds.
Young Lanval never makes demands
So the poor knight has got no credit
Which makes him anxious, low in spirits.
My lords, pray do not feel surprise;
A stranger often lacks advice
When he leaves home to go abroad –
He knows not where to ask for aid.

Lanval, the knight whose tale I tell,
Who served his lord and King so well
Harnesses his destrier
And takes a ride, one sunny day,
To blow the cobwebs clean away.
Concentrating on his riding
He leaves the city far behind him
To canter through the flowery pastures.
He halts, dismounts by flowing waters.

His horse is trembling hard, and flicks
Its ears. Its muscles start to twitch
From an intolerable itch.
"Every good boy deserves a scratch!"
Lanval slackens off the girth

To let him roll on cool green earth
In ecstasy, to rub his back.

His master, too, needs to relax;
Rolling his cloak up as a pillow
He lies at ease there in the meadow,
Still preoccupied with woe.
Even the rippling of the burn
Can't change his mind's dejected turn.
He's melancholy, introspective
Without ambition or objective
He sees no happy prospect. If
He only knew!

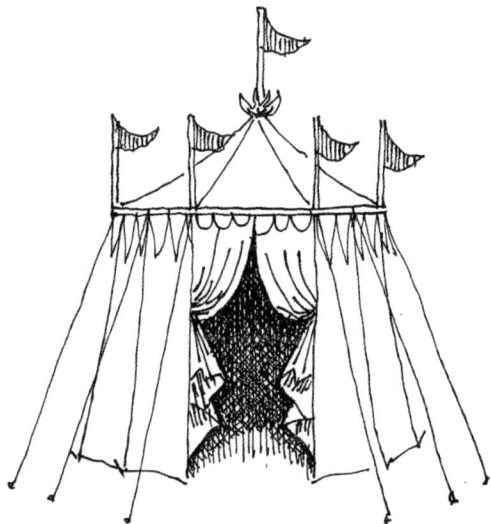

              Along the river
Two lovely women walk together
Dressed in robes of crimson silk.
Lanval has never seen their like.
Each wears a gown that's tightly laced
To emphasise a slender waist.
The first one holds a pair of basins
Fit for an emperor to wash in,
Craftsman-made of purest gold –
This is the truth, as I was told

And I will make no disavowal.
The second lady bears a towel.

They walk directly up to Lanval
As if they had intent to meet him.
A well-bred knight, he stands to greet them.
The damsels are the first to speak.
They have a message to repeat:

"Good Sir Lanval; our lady fair,
The noble, wise and debonair
Sent us ahead to find you here.
She wishes you to come to her.
Walk with us, please. It isn't far
And we will safely guide you there.
Look - in that field you'll see her tent."

So, in a daze, Sir Lanval went.
To his horse, he pays no heed,
But leaves it grazing in the mead.
They lead him to the canopy
Craftsman-made, and fine to see.

Queen Semiramis, in her heyday
That wealthy, puissant, learned lady,
No, nor the emperor Octavian
Could buy one part of that pavilion.
On top, there shines a golden finial
Cast in the likeness of an eagle;
Such priceless guy-ropes; splendid poles
To take the strain of the tent's walls.
I cannot reckon up the whole –
It's worth more than its weight in gold.
There is no monarch under heaven
Not among the dead or living
Who could afford that rare pavilion.

The tent is open, to disclose
A damsel. Summer's first-born rose,
The whitest lily flower that blows –

Her beauty puts them in eclipse
So white her face, so red her lips.
She lies there on a sumptuous couch
(The coverlets would cost as much
As a king's castle) clad in a shift
A simple linen underdress
So finely woven that it left
Little for young Lanval to guess.

Her form is elegant and perfect.
This is beauty without defect.
A cloak of costly ermine fur,
Velvet-lined with deep rich pur-
-ple silk of Alexandria;
This wrap she has thrown over her
To keep her fair skin from the glare
Of the bright sun.
                It does not hide
The lovely curve along her side
Nor the absolute perfection
Of that radiant complexion.
Her face and throat, her neck and bosom
Are whiter than the hawthorn blossom.

The knight, after some hesitation
Goes in, at the maiden's invitation,
And there he sits beside the bed.
"Lanval," she says "My handsome friend
For you I left my own homeland;
On your repute, I journeyed far.
If you are, as they say you are,
A gallant, courtly, worthy knight
You'll have good fortune and delight
Surpassing emperors, counts and kings.
I love you above everything."

Love strikes a sharp spark in his breast
His heart with fire is possessed.
"Beauty, if it is your pleasure
And I am granted such a treasure

As to be desired by you
In love –
        fair lady, I will do
Any deed you bid me to
Wise or foolish, sweet or sour
As long as it is in my power.

"You only have to ask me once
And henceforward I'll renounce
All other earthly fealty
Of human love and loyalty.
To remain with you, faithfully
To love and serve you as your squire,
Is my poor humble heart's desire."

Hearing this ardent declaration
Of love, without prevarication,
This mysterious fair lady
Forthwith yields both heart and body.
Now Lanval's on the royal road!

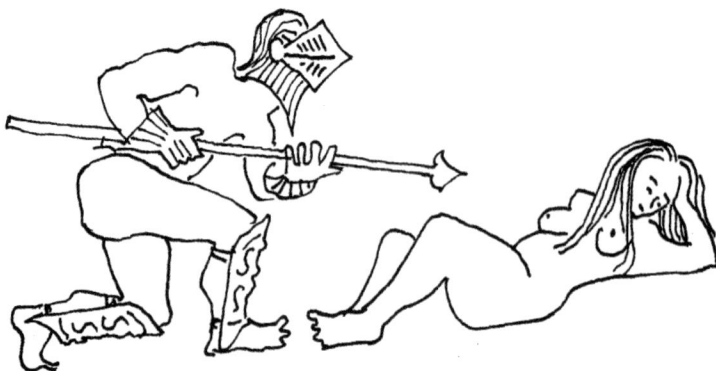

In the sweet moments afterward
She grants the knight a fairy gift: -
He might have everything he wished.
How ever much he gives or spends
She will recompense her friend.
Now he's lodged in a pleasant dwelling.

You might say young Lanval is well in
However prodigal his spending
More gold and silver will roll in.

"Dear friend," she says "I must entreat you
Implore, command, bid and beseech you
On our true love, I beg you, swear
Never to tell our secret, dear,
Or, to speak plain, I'll disappear.
If people learn of our amour
Then you will never see me more
Or have me as your paramour
To have, to cherish and to hold."

Lanval agrees to what he's told
And swears to all that she has said.
He lies beside her on the bed.
Yes, Lanval's in a cushy number.
And so they lie, but do not slumber
All afternoon, until the evening.

Lanval does not think of leaving
He'd rather stay the whole night through –
Providing she allows him to.

"Darling," she says "Get up, my dear
For you can bide no longer here!
You must be gone, while I must stay.
But I've one other thing to say:-

"If you should wish to talk with me
No matter wheresoe'er you be
There is no place you can conceive
Where man may not enjoy his love
Without reproach or hint of shame,
Where I, your true love, cannot come
And do whatever you require
To accomplish your desire.
To all but you, I am invisible;
Likewise, my voice is quite inaudible."

Overjoyed with what she said
He kisses her, and leaves the bed.
The maids who led him to the tent
Dress him in the richest garments;
When he appears in this new raiment
No land or nation on the earth
Can show so handsome, fine a youth.
He is not stupid, or uncouth,
His wits are sharp, his manners proper,
No dullard he, and no clodhopper.
He washes in the golden bowl
And dries his hands on the white towel.

There's food. He eats there, by his mistress.
With such a feast, he's quite resistless.
The damsels serve him courteously
He dines as merry as can be.
There is one dish, a special treat
That's luscious, delicate and sweet
Which Lanval most desires to eat:
For he may shower her with kisses
And hold her close in warm embraces.

But now the maidens clear the table
And lead his horse out from the stable
Correctly harnessed up and saddled.
Such hospitality!
          "Farewell."

He mounts, and rides off to Carlisle.
How often Lanval looks behind;
This strange adventure haunts his mind
Wild and anxious thoughts assail him
And his courage almost fails him.
He's thrown into complete confusion
Was it all true, or an illusion?

At his lodgings, he's amazed
To see his serving-men well dressed.

That night, his lavish hospitality
Became the talk of the locality.
No-body knew how he afforded it.
His critics talked of how he lorded it.

No knight who lacked accommodation
No matter his poor lowly station
But Lanval heard about his plight
Invited him to spend the night
And served him like a gentleman.
Lanval gave with open hand
Lanval freed captives from their bonds
Lanval clothed rogues and vagabonds
Lanval became the jongleurs' friend.

Lanval's charity knew no end
He soon became the guardian angel
To everybody, friend or stranger.
And meanwhile, to his great delight
Whether morning, noon or night
He frequently may see his dear –
He simply calls, and she appears.

* * *

If my memory is clear
After St. John's Day, that same year,
About thirty noble knights
Take the fresh air for their delight
At ease in the garden round the tower
Where Arthur's Queen sits in her bower.

Among them was the count Gawain
With his handsome cousin, Ywain.
Up spoke Gawain, whose affability
Made him beloved by all the gentry:

"By heavens, lords, this is a slight!
We have forgotten to invite
Our friend Lanval, that gallant knight

Who is so liberal in giving.
His father is a wealthy king.
I'm sure Lanval should be here, too."
So back went the whole retinue
To Lanval's digs. The merry crew
Winkled him out to join the fun.

In a window, sat the Queen
With three of her tiring-women.
As she looked out through the lancet
Of fine-cut stone, her gaze just chanced to
Glimpse the company on the lawn.
All the King's men.
                    There is Lanval.
A splendid knight. And her eyes dwell
Upon him. So she turns to call
One of her ladies: "Send for our maidens –
Pick the most cultured, finely made ones
To come and join us in the gardens
And enjoy the height of summer."

The courtly damsels, each a stunner,
Thirty or more descend the stair
Onto the lawn to take the air
Gracefully wandering at leisure.
The gallants' faces beam with pleasure
As they turn their steps to meet them.
Courteously, they bow and greet them
Hold hands in courtly conversation
Urbane and charming recreation.

Yet Lanval lingers, steps aside
Goes to a quiet spot and hides
Far from the chatter of the crowd.
Even a courtly laugh's too loud
For he is champing at the bit
To embrace his heart's delight
To hold and kiss, to touch and savour.
All other joys have lost their flavour.
Lanval disdains his fellows' pleasure

If he can't enjoy his treasure.

The Queen, who sees him all alone
Briskly walks across the lawn.
She sits beside him in the arbour
Tells him the fancies that disturb her–

"Sir Lanval, greatly I esteem you
Love you, honour you, and deem you
A verray parfit gentil knight.
You may have all for your delight!
Just tell me what you want of me
You have my love.
                    Make love with me.
It is your privilege to have me
And with due joy, make me your own."

"Madame," he begs, "Leave me alone!
I feel no stir of love for you –
Nor am I ever likely to.
For a long time I've served the King
I never would prove false to him;
Neither for your sake, nor your passion
Would I betray him in this fashion!"

At this, the Queen flies off the handle
Initiating a huge scandal.
She utters the first spiteful thought
That's in her head:
                    "I know your sort!
It's common gossip in the court
You've other outlets for your sport.
Of course you've never fancied women –
You've got a bunch of hand-picked yeomen!
You slake your infamous desires
With pretty serving boys and squires.
Why did you ever turn up here
You snivelling, skulking, craven queer!
King Arthur's spotless reputation
Is tarnished by association.

I even fear for his salvation!
God sees the company he keeps
With such a sinful little creep."

She, who enjoys a pampered rich life
Harangues him like a common fishwife!
Her outburst shakes him to the heart.
He snaps back with a quick retort
But in his anger's flaming heat
Says things he later will regret.
I never saw an uglier scene
This good knight with this screaming Queen.

"Listen, lady, my activities
Do not extend to those proclivities
I don't indulge forbidden liberties.
I love, and am loved in return
By one whose charms and beauties earn
Honour above all other women
I have known.
                    I'll tell you this
So listen well, and watch my lips –
Any of her serving wenches,
Even the one who scrubs the dishes,
Surpasses you, Queen, in her grace,
Figure, complexion, pretty face
In learning and integrity."

Barely maintaining dignity
She flounces off, back to her tower
And there she weeps for several hours,
Wretched with misery and rage.
Such impudent recrimination –
Time young Lanval was taught his station.
She takes to her bed, in desperation
Pleading a strange indisposition:
She will not rise again, unless
The King exacts condign redress
For Sir Lanval's grave affront.

The King's home from a thrilling hunt
Out in the woods of his domain.
He climbs the tower to see the Queen.
When he comes in, she makes a scene:
Starts to lament, complain, entreat
And throws herself at Arthur's feet.
In frenzied histrionic passion
She begs his Majesty's compassion:

"Lanval has brought dishonour on me
By forcing his attentions on me!
When I gave him a stern rebuff
He said the most disgusting stuff!

"As if that insult weren't enough
He started saying something monstrous
Bragging that he has a mistress
Who is so virtuous and wise
Such noble birth, such sparkling eyes.

"He'd rather have her lowest skivvy!
Even the slut who cleans the privy
Is worthier of high esteem
Than I am! I, who am
                    Your Queen!"

The King is full of righteous wrath
And swears, on his most solemn oath:
If Lanval can't, as law allows,
Defend himself, he's for the gallows
Or death by burning at the stake.
That's how you scotch a treacherous snake.
Out of the chamber Arthur storms
Calls his three most beefy barons
And sends them to arrest the knight.

* * *

Lanval, despairing of his plight,
Has gone back to his rooms to mourn

Convinced his lady won't return.
Now he has lost her through his bragging, he
Castigates himself in agony
For breaking faith with his true lover.
He calls her name, over and over
Quite hopelessly. She does not answer.

Lanval weeps and sighs and groans
Falls to the floor in deathly swoons;
Then, when he wakes, he cries forgiveness
For his betrayal of his mistress.
He curses his impetuousness,
His reckless tongue, his heart itself.
By grace he did not kill himself.

However loud his lamentation
Or deep his self-recrimination
Or humble are his pleas for grace
He never more will see her face.
What shall become of poor Lanval?
Down, and arise he never shall.

Three sheriffs burst into his suite
"Now then, my lad, up on your feet!
You're summonsesed to court, toot sweet!!"

The King has ordered his arrest
At the Queen's express behest.
She makes the gravest allegation.
He's led away;
                his protestation
From the depths of his despair –
Why don't they kill him then and there?
For him, life isn't worth a thing.

So Lanval's brought before the King.
He stands there mute in his dejection
Silenced by sad recollection.
His misery is plain to see.
The King harangues him angrily:

"Wretch, you have wronged me grievously!
And instigated a base scheme
To slander me and shame the Queen
With crude defamatory lies.
Your boastful folly was unwise.
You praised your mistress to the skies –
She must be quite a prodigy
If she's all she's cracked up to be!
The noblest creature in the world
No less, whose slattern servant-girl
Is lovelier and worthier
Than is the Queen of your seigneur."

One by one, just like a lawyer,
Lanval denies each of the charges:
The harassment the Queen alleges
Intent to wrong and shame King Arthur.
Yet he concedes a point, and further
Testifies there is one truth –
                              "Oh
Yes, I boasted of my lover;
Because of this, she's gone forever.
And now, my lords, I will agree
To do what you require of me
In recompense for any damage."

At this, the King, still much enraged
Calls his whole entourage of knights
To arbitrate on what is right,
Lest history should judge him harshly
And blame him for abuse of mastery.

His courtiers are a loyal throng
Who follow Arthur, right or wrong.
They all debate it, and decide
There's an indictment to be tried.
They set the day. Till then, meanwhile
It is the duty of Lanval
To find a sponsor to stand bail

And warrant he'll attend the trial.
By then, the company at court
Will be increased and reinforced
By the return of far-off peers;
Many have gone to fight the wars –
Including Britain's finest minds.
Just household knights are left behind.

Back to the King, the men of court
Go to present their full report.
The King demands good proofs of surety.
Now Lanval feels his insecurity;
He is forlorn, alone and friendless
Far from his parents, poor and landless.

Gawain steps forward, pledges money.
Then his companions.   One by one, they
Vouch for Lanval.
              The King decrees
"Each man of you who guarantees
Pledges all fiefdoms, lands and fees
Held from the crown. Securities
I will exact in total forfeit
From each of you who bails him out,
If base Lanval evades the law."

The pledge is made. The knights withdraw,
Escorting Lanval to his quarters.
They castigate his dismal thoughts, as
These will lead to grave affliction.
"A curse on lunatic affection!"
"Excess of love is stupid folly.
Life is too short for melancholy!"
They call in every day, to check
For signs of self-harm or neglect.
Is he eating? Is he drinking?
At risk of suicide, they're thinking.

On the trial's appointed day
The peers arrive in full array
The King and Queen lead the procession
Which makes a dignified impression.
The Table Round in plenary session
In the full majesty of law
Strikes every Briton's heart with awe.

Lanval, led by his guarantors
Enters the court. His friends are sad
For things are looking very bad.
I think a hundred, if not more
Would do whatever's in their power
To free him from the trumped-up charges
And bogus crimes the Queen alleges.

The King requires a verdict, based
According to the law's due process,
On full assessment of the case
Submitted by the prosecution
With the defendant's refutation.
The jury's out.

                    The matter stands
Entirely in their lordships' hands.
The peers, in solemn, sombre state
Assemble to deliberate.
The outcome utterly depends
On their decision. They're concerned
That such a good and noble stranger,
While in their midst, should come to danger.
Yet some still wish to bring him down
To gratify the vengeful crown.

The Speaker, Earl of Cornwall,
States:
                    "Our stern duty, without fail,
Is to see right and truth prevail
No matter what we think or feel
Deep in our hearts. King Arthur's vassal
(Well known to all as Sir Lanval)
Is charged by the King with these misdeeds
To which the knight makes counter-pleas:-

"Vaunting the beauty of his mistress
To the Queen's wrath, and deep distress.

"Yet no-one but the King makes charges –
To my mind, we should disregard these,
For any man of common sense
Doubts unsupported evidence.
However, in this case, we must
Remember we've a sacred trust
Towards our sovereign lord the King
To honour him in everything.
We will fulfil our solemn troth
By binding Lanval on his oath –
Then, let the plaintiff furnish proof.

"But if the lady will come forward
To verify his every word
And she's as lovely as he said;
Why then, the Queen will be appeased
(And I, for one, will be well pleased).
She will show Sir Lanval mercy –
He did not speak maliciously.

"But if he can't corroborate
Every detail that he states,
Then there can be no more debate:
We must make our meaning plain
That Sir Lanval can't remain
In the King's service one more day.
He is dismissed, and sent away."

Their message to Lanval requests
That he call, in his own defence,
To be a guarantor and witness
Exhibited as evidence
In person, in the court –
                        his mistress.
He tells them this demand is hopeless
Calls for her aid would be quite fruitless.
The message-bearer comes back running
To tell them help is not forthcoming.
The King speeds their deliberations
– His Queen is waiting in impatience.

Just as they rise to give their findings
They see two maids approach them, riding
At ladies' pace on two fine palfreys,
Their garments floating in the breeze;
Over their naked flesh they wear
Fine crimson silk, as light as air.
The knights gaze at this pair of charmers
And pop the rivets in their armour.
No wonder they are pleased to see them
– Surely they're witnesses to free him!

Four of Lanval's band of brothers
His friend Sir Gawain, with three others,
Run up to Lanval, tug his sleeve
"Look, here's a sight you won't believe –
Two lovely damsels. Come on, please!
Surely your lady's one of these!"

"No." he replies. "She is not there.
Neither of them's my lady fair.
I have no notion who they are
From whence they come, who sent them here,
Whither they go – I know not where."

All this while, the maids, still riding
Approach them, passing right beside them,
Till they arrive at Arthur's seat
Dismounting at his highness' feet
Before the British royal throne.
Each fairer than a rose full-blown
With speech of dulcet courtly tone:

"King, prepare your state apartments
Deck them with sumptuous appointments.
We come ahead to make arrangements
For our lady when she comes
An honoured guest to Arthur's home.
Drape silken hangings round the bed
Where our fair mistress lays her head."

Arthur assents with warmth and grace;
They shall be welcome in the palace.
Two trusted knights are harbingers
To show them to the suite of chambers.

A silence falls there in the court.
"My lords!" calls Arthur. "Your report!
Perhaps, because of this excitement
You have forgotten the indictment.
Give your decision on this case
Which, we've no doubt, is firmly based
On diligent deliberation
Of the learned prosecution
And the pleas in mitigation.
We warn you, lords, you face our rage
If there are any more delays.
How many hours have we waited!"

"Sire," they say, "We have debated
But our opinion is divided
The matter is yet undecided.
We think the court should reconvene
Considering those girls we've seen
So lovely, gracious and serene."

The peers assemble, deep in thought
And mutters rumble round the court.
They're arguing amongst themselves
But soon, all quarrelling is shelved –

Lo and behold, two charming girls
Riding on good Spanish mules
And clad in Phrygian silk dresses
Which drape their bodies like caresses,
Are coming through the entranceway.

The knights and vassals shout "Hooray!"
(No doubt thinking: "Two more beauts
With all the damsel attributes.")

They tell each other that their pal
The admirable knight Lanval
Is free, and safely off the hook.
You only have to take one look.

Now it's Ywain's turn to tell him
So, with his friends, he runs up yelling:
"My lord, rejoice, we have great news.
For heaven's sake, speak to us, please!
Here are two lovely maidens coming
Enchanting, elegant, quite stunning.
We know your lady must be one of 'em!"

Lanval quickly interjects;
He can, by no means, recollect
Or recognise them. His affection
Does not run in that direction.

The damsels ride right past the knights
Up to the throne, where they alight.
The crowd unanimously praises
Their curves, complexion and sweet faces –
Fairer than was the Queen, in truth,
Even in her first flush of youth.

The elder's speech is clear and wise,
"King, we are here to supervise
The preparation of the room;
Our lady mistress will soon come
For her audience with you."
The chamberlains escort the two
Upstairs to join the other damsels.
They do not heed the patient mules
Who are consigned to trusty grooms
While they're attending to the rooms.

Again, his Majesty requires
The final judgement of the peers.
They've taken too much time about it;
The Queen's out of her mind about it

How dare they keep her Highness waiting!
So, a third time, the jury meets.
But –

      who's this coming down the street?

Alone, on horseback, rides a girl
The rarest beauty in the world.
A fine white palfrey bears her sweetly
His gleaming hooves are pacing gently;
An arching neck, a fine-boned head
In every point a thoroughbred
His eyes are bright, teeth white and even
The rarest Arab under heaven
And fit to carry such a mistress.
As for the value of his harness –
Such that no emperor or lord
Could, in his wildest dreams, afford
Short of selling all his lands
Or putting them in usurers' hands.

As for the lady's dress –
                Ah, she
Wears classical simplicity
The choicest pure-white linen shift
Whose seams are laced instead of stitched.
From arm to hem, at right and left
The lady's bare sides are revealed
– Her lissom figure, slender haunches –
Why should such beauty be concealed?

The freshest snowfall on the branches
Of a wood of silver birches
Is less white than her dazzling face is.
Her bright eyes gleam with liveliness;
A lovely mouth, a nose well-set;
Brown eyebrows and a handsome forehead;
A pale and graceful swan-like neck.

Her blonde hair falls in shining waves –
There never was a sight so brave.

The bright threads in a cloth of gold
Beside her hair, look dull and cold.
She wears a rich dark velvet cape
With soft voluminous folds to drape
Around her body as a wrap.
Upon her wrist, a sparrowhawk,
And at her heel, a greyhound stalks.

All of Carlisle comes out in force
To see a fine lady on a white horse;
The rich and poor, both old and young
To check if the reports were wrong.
When they see her, there's no more laughter.
The jurors think she is a wonder.
From palsied crone to beardless boy
No-one beholds her without joy;
No-one who sees her fails to brighten
Their troubles eased, their burdens lightened.

Up run Sir Lanval's fighting men:
"There is a lady coming, friend, who's
Here, God willing, to defend you.
Just now she's riding through the town
Her hair's not mousy, or nut-brown.
In beauty, she's a paragon
Above all other earthly women."

Again Sir Lanval lifts his head
Again expects to be misled;
Then, with a sigh, he blushes red,
Stammers, cries out eagerly:

"Now, by my faith, yes, it is she!
Let law exact its penalty
If she will show no mercy on me
I care not what I must endure –
To see her face shall be my cure."

She passes through the castle door
Where none so fair has passed before;

There she dismounts before the throne.
Then, in the sight of everyone,
She lets her cloak fall to the floor.
The throng is struck quite dumb with awe.
King Arthur, in his gallantry,
Rises to honour the fair lady;
His knights make their polite obeisance
And swear to be her faithful servants.
Now all the court has seen her closely
And rings with praises of her beauty.

Having no wish to linger here
The lady speaks out, calm and clear:
"King, I have loved one of your vassals
And this is he, your knight Lanval
Who stands arraigned here, in this hall.
I can't let harm fall on his head
Simply for those rash words he said.

"For know, King, that your Queen speaks slander –
He never laid a finger on her
Or by a single word or glance
Implored her Highness for romance.

"Of the bold boast he made of me
Let me acquit him instantly;
He's innocent, as you can see,
And all your peers and knights agree!"

The King consents to let things be
In line with the judges' resolution.
A unanimous solution
The verdict's simple, quick and painless –
Lanval's character is stainless!
The court at once declares him free.
But where can Lanval's truelove be?
Although the King begged her to stay
She and her maids have gone away.

Outside the hall, there is a block

Of solid dark-grained granite rock;
The heavy horseman in their armour
Mount their chargers from this stair.
Light-footed Lanval leaps up there
To look and see if he can find her.
Through the door of the great hall, she
Comes out riding on her palfrey.

One bound, and Lanval is behind her.
Off goes the horse, with his two riders
Swiftly away to Avalon –
Which, according to the Britons
Is a fair and fruitful isle –
Thither, the lady has beguiled
Sir Lanval.

     And there he will stay
Enjoying endless golden days –
I'm told he never came away.
No news, and nothing more to say
So here's an ending to my lai.

VI LES DEUS AMANZ : *The Two Sweet Young Things*

In Normandy, in days of old
Occurred a tale that's often told
Of two young souls who loved so madly
That their adventure turned out sadly.
Their tragic story touched the Bretons
Who made this lai, *Les Deus Amanz*.

You can still find, in Normandy
(Known as Neustria in their day)
A mountain of prodigious size –
Right on its top, their tomb still lies.
Beneath it, at the king's command
Was a strong city, finely planned.
He was the lord of all the land
And nation of the Pitrians
Therefore, he called his city Pitres.
With many a handsome house and street
The town is standing to this day
(I recommend a weekend stay).
Around the handsome citadel
Is countryside we all know well
Along the valley of the Seine –
Le Val de Pitres is its name.

The widowed king has no heirs male;
His only offspring is a girl
The heroine of this sad tale.
She's courtly, sweet and beautiful
The only comfort of his soul
And single object of his love
Now that his wife has passed above.
Many of his staff and ministers
Find his devotion to her sinister
They blame the king, and some reprove him.
Their stern reproaches shame and move him.

So the old king sat down and planned

How any suitors for her hand
Might be forestalled. Then he can have her
Entirely to himself forever.
So it's proclaimed both far and near :
"All hopefuls should get one thing clear:
It is decided and decreed
All claimants must perform this deed
A rigorous and stringent test:-
Without a pause for breath or rest
He must climb up the lofty mountain
Carrying the lovely maiden
In his arms, and never falter
If he would wed her at the altar."

When the news spreads through the land
Many decide to try their hand
At this absurd and pointless deed.
No man Jacques of them succeeds.
Some of them, by gallant struggle,
Get half way up before they stumble –
Without the strength for one step further
Their brave attempt to win is over.
When it was known the task was hopeless
No man paid court to the princess.

Well, a young fellow lives nearby,
A count's son, pleasing to the eye
Noble and decent, with ambition
By splendid feats to gain position
And to cement his place at court,
His only cultural resort.
He visits often. There he sought
To woo the princess, whom he loved.
Would she agree to be betrothed
And to return his tenderness
Deeper than mere words express?
Because he has her father's favour
For he is handsome, courtly, brave, her
Heart is willing, and she's glad
And proud to love this charming lad.

They meet as often as they can
To talk together, and to plan
A happy future. They conceal
The ardent passions that they feel
From all potential spying eyes –
Even their tears of grief, their sighs.
Their suffering was so intense!
Yet the young man thinks it good sense
To bear their sorrows for a while
Rather than haste their love, and fail.
His love's the cause of great distress
So he goes off to see his mistress
Who is so lovely, good and wise.
He begs, lamenting on his knees:

"Let's run away, my darling, please –
This is a risk we both must take.
I can no longer stand this ache!
If I should ask your father's blessing
To take his most adored possession
I know he'd never let us marry
Unless I pass the test to carry
You in my arms up to the summit.
The prospect makes my spirits plummet."

"My love" says she, "I know full well
This is one challenge you would fail
You haven't got the strength and fitness.
Yet I am sure, as God's my witness,
My father's anger would be pitiless.
If we eloped, his grief and rage
Would eat his heart out all his days.
I love him so, the dear old man,
I'll keep him happy if I can.
To cause him hurt is inconceivable –
Our future's not yet irretrievable.
Now, listen, for I've planned it out.

"In Italy, I have an aunt

A dame of substance and of parts
With her help, things will turn out happily.
At Salerno University
(You go straight on through Napoli)
She's studied all the healing arts
For thirty years, from learned masters.
She knows the salves, the brews, the plasters
Charms, herbs and roots and magic potions
Brought from far lands and distant oceans.

"If you're prepared to travel there
I'll write a letter you can bear
To introduce yourself to her.
When once you tell her of our plight
She'll give you all the help she might
With good advice and tender care.
I'm sure you can depend on her.

"She will prescribe you distillations
Tinctures, tonics, medications
That will bring comfort, lend you strength
And get you into shape.
                    At length
When you return, ask for my hand
And, if things go as I have planned,
My father, thinking you a stripling
And physically quite a weakling,
Will gladly read you the decree
Whereby no man may marry me
Save the one who can carry me
Held in his arms, up to the top
With never a breather, or a stop."

Such clever, witty, wise advice -
The girl's not just a pretty face.
This puts new heart into the lad:
"Thanks, darling, I'd be very glad
Of any nostrum of your aunt's.
Your blessing, please. I'll leave at once!"
He rushes home to pack and plan

The journey out, as best he can.
He'll take a modest baggage train –
Only his most trusted men,
His finest clothes, a deal of moneys,
Palfreys to ride, and good pack-ponies.
It's a long journey that he's making
A truly massive undertaking
But he's too love-sick to despond.
He pores over the mappemonde:-

"All the way from Normandy
Across the Alps to Italy
Then, somewhere south of Napoli –
Salerno."
　　　How he hopes that he
Will find material help and counsel
From the aunt of his dear damsel.

They reach the aunt's house with good speed.
"Your niece sends greetings. Here, please read."
She reads intently, from the top
Right to the end. Sizing him up,
The aunt invites the youth to stop
With her.
　　　"You're such a slender chap
A little half-starved whippet pup!
Drink this, my dear, to build you up.
It's potent stuff – a single swig
Will make you lively as a grig!"

With a mystic incantation
She stirs a complex preparation
Of elixirs and macerations
With healing herbs from far off nations.
Many young men swear by this potion.
However weakened by exhaustion
Bowed down by burdens or affliction
Depressed in spirits by emotion
And the anguish of the soul –
This medicine will make him whole.

By the powers of cabbalism
It restores the organism
Acting through the venous system
From the beating of the heart
It circulates to every part
Right to the marrow of the bones!
Here's an end to sighs and moans.
It's a fast-acting remedy
One sip, then – farewell malady.

He rides back to his native soil
With the potion in a phial.
Though he's delighted to be home
He doesn't dawdle there for long
But rushes off to see the king.

"I beg you for your daughter's hand.
Believe me sir, I understand
The task that I must undertake
To prove myself a worthy mate.
I'll carry her, in these my arms,
Up to the top, no fear of harm."

His majesty did not forbid it,
Yet, I believe, considered it
Madness in one so very young
– And, in appearance, far from strong –
When sturdy citizens had failed.
No valiant heart had yet prevailed;
Brave, tough and wise men all gave up
Before they reached the mountain top.

He sets the day for his attempt
No knight or bondsman is exempt
All of his friends and neighbours come –
No-one is left at home, not one.
When folk hear of this event
No invitation need be sent!
The people pour into the town
From the regions all around.
A princess, carried by her swain
Across mountainous terrain
Could you resist it?
                    Nor could they!

In preparation for the day
The girl, to make it easy for him,
Resolves to keep herself in trim.
To make assurance doubly sure

She undertakes a diet cure
And starves herself as if for Lent,
Like the most zealous penitent.

Oh, the poor princess, what folly!
Now girls, don't ever be so silly.
Worries about how slim you are
Bring anorexia or bulimia.
Perhaps you will agree with me
That here's a tragic irony.
He loved her for herself entire
Aflame with youthful wild desire
For her sweet soft voluptuous curves.
And she loved him, all bones and nerves;
Though physically he's ineffectual
He is a true French intellectual.
An intellectual's always gaunt
(And I'm – one of the few that aren't).

On the anticipated morning
He rises as the day is dawning;
The first arrival at the start
With apprehension in his heart.
Despite his welter of emotion
He has made sure to bring the potion.

Along the valley of the Seine
All through the throng that crowds the plain
His highness leads the young princess.
Choosing the simplest, lightest dress
She's wearing nothing but her shift.

She's up in his arms, so slight to lift.
He, knowing that she'll not deceive him
Gives her the tonic for safe-keeping.
By evening, she will be his wife
And so he trusts her with his life.

But, ah my dears, I have a notion
He'll gain no profit from the potion
For youth knows no restraint or caution
When in the grip of deep emotion.
Middle age brings moderation
And a true sense of proportion –
At least, friends, that's what I've been told.
The young think first love won't grow cold
And hope to die before they get old.

He's off, at high velocity
And up the first stretch with alacrity
To the first mark, quick as can be.
He can't believe it. He's halfway!
He's so thrilled that he doesn't think
About the flask of magic drink.

But she can hear that he sounds puffed.
"Darling!" she urges "Take a draught!
I can feel your strength is flagging
Take a sip, please, from the flacon.
Health and vigour are imparted."

"Dearest, I feel – puff – quite strong-hearted.
While I can still take three steps forward
My no means will I rest or stop,
Not even for a – tiny sip!
Once the masses see me pause

They'll deafen me – with groans and roars
It would be – dreadfully off-putting
And I'd be sure to lose – my footing!
I can't afford – to break my stride
Or I will stumble, slip and slide.
Please – honey – no more interruptions."

Onward he climbs the lofty mountain.
Now they're two thirds of the way up
He's quite done in and fit to drop
But somehow, just keeps on his legs.
Over and over, how she begs:
"Darling, please, darling, take your drink!"
But he can barely hear or think.
In fact, he chooses not to hear
Or to believe his anxious dear.

No, he will do this thing alone
Prove to himself that he is strong.
In agony, he struggles on.
A few more steps, and he has done it.
At last, he makes it to the summit.
But he's incurred such grievous strain
And suffered such appalling pain
He slumps, and does not rise again.
A fluttering within his chest
And then–
           his heart flees from his breast.

The princess sees her fallen lover.
He's fainted, and will soon recover.
She kneels beside him, tries to slip
The potion-flask between his lips.
"Speak to me, darling!"
                        He cannot
For he was dead before he dropped.
In grief, she gives a piteous wail
And hurls away the precious phial
Sprinkling the magic potion
Over the herbage of the mountain

Watering the barren earth
And engendering rebirth.
So potent was its growing power
That many a healing herb and flower
Took root there, having been well-nourished;
There, to this day, they grow and flourish
And you may pick them, for good health.

Ah, but I forget myself.
Now I must tell of the poor maid
Who has lost her bonny lad.
Her grief has driven her quite mad. She
Lies beside his poor, racked body
Clasping him in wild embraces
Showering eyes and lips with kisses;
With her pale forefinger she traces
Each loved feature of his face.
Grief for his anguish breaks her heart
And she expires there, on the spot.
So ends the life of this princess
In all her sweet wise loveliness.

When the couple don't appear
The king, and all those waiting there,
Are anxious, and make up their minds
To follow, and look out for signs.
Alas, we know what they will find.
The king collapses on the ground.
When he recovers from his swoon
He grieves aloud with howls and cries.
None of the strangers is dry-eyed.
For three whole days the hills resound
With the lamentable sound
Vast crowds of mourners gather round
While the two lie there on the ground.
On the fourth day, they are entombed
In a fine marble mausoleum
There, on the summit of the mountain
Where, so they say, you can still see them.

Then, the throng turns for the descent.
In solitude, the king laments,
And, for all I know, repents.

Thus ends the tale of the ordeal
Of two who died in time of trial.
For the young lovers' sad romance
The mountain's called *Les Deus Amanz*.
It came about just as I say
And Breton singers made this lai.

VII YONEC : *The Lai of the Hawk*

Since writing lais is my vocation
I shall pursue my occupation
With diligence. There'll be no falling
Off in commitment to my calling.
I hereby pledge myself to tell
All the adventures I know well
And rhyme them with due elegance
– Or my name's not Marie de France!

Now a longing seizes me
To tell a tale that pleases me
Of long ago. Here you shall learn
How a fine young man was born,
The strange adventure of his father
And how he met this young man's mother.
The father's named Muldumarec.
This ancient lai is called *Yonec*.

In Britain lived, as I was told,
A man rich in both land and gold
Tight-fisted, cruel and very old
His motto "What I have, I hold."
And what he held – came from the Church!
No-one would knock him off his perch
As God's official at Caërwent
In Monmouthshire (or is it Gwent?).

His agents gathered tithes and rents
From burgesses within the town
And fiefdoms in the country round;
Stole harbour-duties from the crown
And sought for cargoes to impound
From vessels on the River Düelas
Where, in those days, large ships could pass
 – Though no-one now knows where it was.
His set-up's like the Sheriff of Nottingham's.

A nasty bastard. Hope God's rotting him!
Although he was far gone in years
He thought it wise to get some heirs
And offspring to consolidate
The assets of his great estate.
So he decided to get wed
And take some nubile lass to bed.

His chosen bride was young and lovely
Wise, highly born, sweet-natured, courtly.
Her parents dealt their daughter cheap;
Ah, lords and ladies, I could weep
That she should marry one so old
For land, inheritance and gold.
Despite her frantic tears and pleading
She is disposed as stock for breeding.
Her youth and beauty are degraded
Her precious innocence is traded
To one whose appetites are jaded.

Her beauty has him quite besotted
Yet he's too sly to play the dotard;
Because she is so fair and wise
And so refined, her husband tries
To keep her from lascivious eyes.
Like every man of wealth and power
He has a bastion and tower.
There, in a great dank stone-slabbed room,
In echoing chill and Stygian gloom
His wife is sealed as in a tomb.

The old king has an ancient sister,
A lonely widow. He enlists her
To be a stringent moral guard
And keep her on the righteous path.
There were some other women there
Living in a room elsewhere;
His wife's forbidden to address them
Without her guardian's permission.

She's pent up seven years or more
And all this time she never bore
A child, for it was quite apparent
That their union was barren.
She cannot leave to see her friends
Or family. Nor can her parents
Visit their poor captive daughter.
Bed-times, no chamberlain or porter
Dares to climb the stair and enter
Before his lord, to light the candle,
Lest he's suspected of a scandal.

Perpetual sorrow racks the lady;
With every tear, her beauty fades. She
Loses hope and self-respect
And suffers every dire effect
Of total, abject self-neglect.
This pitiful imprisoned wife
Prays for a swift end to her life.

In April time, the merry spring
When all the birds begin to sing
His lordship rises with the dawn
And puts his hunting habit on.
He rousts his sister from her lie-in
To lock and bar the doors behind him
The toothless crone obeys him, whining.
Off to the forest he goes riding
Hounds and huntsmen all beside him.

The old hag's footsteps slowly falter
As off she totters with her psalter
To recite some pious texts –
Comminatory prayers and collects –
Leaving the lady all alone
To weep, to sigh, bewail and moan.

After a fretful sleepless night
She stares into the brilliant light
From the high lancet. One bright beam

Slants downward in a golden stream.
Now she is left quite solitary
She may indulge the luxury
Of a forlorn soliloquy.

"Why was I born to this hard fate?
My husband, whom I loathe and hate
Has me defenceless in his power
Locked up in this appalling tower.
Alas, I'll gain my liberty
Only when death has taken me
And I am carried to my tomb.
That happy day can't come too soon!

"What madness makes him keep his wife
A wretched prisoner for life?
Why is he jealous in his dotage?
To what mad fear am I a hostage?
Does he enjoy my melancholy?
He must be senile in his folly
Gaga, barking, off his trolley
Deluded, mad and paranoid
To fear that he might be betrayed
If I once saw the light of day!
He will not even let me pass
To go to church and hear the mass.
If I had chance for conversation
And the occasional diversion
I could assume a gracious mask
For him, though it's a lot to ask –
Pretence is such a thankless task.

"I curse my parents, and the priest
The marriage brokers and the rest
Who tied me to this jealous beast
Bound up for ever, flesh to flesh.
Curse every fumbling vile caress!

"Like a tethered nanny-goat
I struggle with a tight, harsh rope

Which will not break.
                    There is no hope
That he might die, for at his birth
And baptism he was immersed
In that dark river under earth
The hellish Styx. Forever curse
That black and frigid flood of hate.
Unlike Achilles, he has got
No single weak or mortal spot.
Hard are his nerves, his tough blood vessels
Pulse with abundant red corpuscles.

"I have heard, in Celtic lais
How often in the olden days
In this fair magic land of Wales
Wonders came to those who wait
For solace in a wretched state.

"Handsome knights in shining armour
Would meet and love some courtly charmer
And ladies find a handsome lover
Cultured, brave and of high honour.
No slur could stain their reputation
For none could see such assignations
Only the lady and her lover
Had eyes to feast on one another
And, to the world, they were invisible.

"Oh, if such wonders once were possible
They might still happen. If they do
I wish, I wish they might come true
And wish again. Dear Lord, help me!
All-conquering God, may such things be."

After this burst of eloquence
The girl looks up from her lament
And heavenwards she lifts her eyes
To catch a small glimpse of the sky
Through the high window.
                    And there falls

A shadow on the grey stone wall.

Where the sunlight sheds its beam
The spectre of a bird is seen
A mighty creature, wings wide spread.
Her heart is chilled with awe and dread
As the bird swoops down, and glides
To stand before her in its pride.
It seems to be a hawk, most splendid
In the glorious prime of plume.
He sheds a glamour through the room.

From his condition, I would guess his
Age at six moults, more or less;
Strapped to his feet, fine leather jesses.
His handsome regal stance expresses
From stream-lined tail to haughty beak
A male goshawk at his peak.

The great bird stands a little space
All the while gazing on her face
And then: -
           begins to shift his shape
Transforming to a handsome knight
Who appears gentle, and polite.
The lady, flushed with sudden fright,
With trembling hands puts on her veil

Adjusts her kerchief to conceal
The utter wonder that she feels.

Who among us, man or woman
In our frailty merely human
Would not be cowed by such an omen?
Can it be some impious warning?
We fear such fetches may well be
From his satanic majesty.
Is the bird-knight an imitation
Angel of annunciation?
This hawk might be a hellish raptor
Seeking mortal souls to capture.
Ah, no. He is, I am convinced
A tercel-gentle for a prince.

* * *

"Lady", he says "Be of good cheer.
There is no need for you to fear
Or cover up your lovely features.
The goshawk is a noble creature.
Though I appear a mystery
Cloaked in charmed obscurity
I swear to you that you may trust me
And I beseech you, lady, love me!

"It's for your sake that I am here
I have loved you for many a year
You are my only true desire.
No other lady has my heart
Nor ever will. And yet my fate
Was to keep distant and to wait.
I could not leave my own country
Until I heard you wish for me.
Now, I may truly be your suitor."

Since his gracious words have soothed her
She lifts her veil to give her answer –
Yes, she consents to be his lover

That is, if he can prove to her
His faith in God. Her full permission
Depends upon a shared religion.
She will love him, or love no other.
His noble beauty's won her over
She's never seen a knight so fine
Nor ever will, in her lifetime.

"My lady, you have spoken fairly.
It's my concern, " he says sincerely
"Never to cause you doubt or fear
By the charmed means that I came here.
Nor would I be the false occasion
Of any doubt or accusation
Against your spotless reputation.

"I worship God of all Creation
Who is our hope and our salvation
From the wretched state of sin
Our father Adam cast us in
From one bite of the bitter fruit.
God's love divides us from the brutes
The flame of life in darkness glimmers
To be a light to all poor sinners
Who wander this sad world in anguish;
This light will never be extinguished.

"If you misdoubt my faith and truth
I undertake to furnish proof.
Send directly for your chaplain
With a message of concern
To say you're ill, and have been stricken
Suddenly by some grave sickness.
You wish to take the bread and wine
Which the Lord of all ordained
To heal poor sinners of their pain.

"I'll cast a spell. Then, to his eyes,
I will appear in your guise
To receive the bread of Christ.

The Christian credo I'll recite
In full. Then you need have no doubt."

She thanks him for the fair words said.
He lies beside her on the bed –
Yet does not touch her, and resists
The wish to clasp her and to kiss.

Now the old dragon has come back
And finds the lady is awake –
"Time to get up! I'll bring your garments."

"No, I'm too ill!" the girl laments
"I feel so dreadfully alarmed –
This pain portends a mortal harm.
Fetch me the chaplain urgently
To pardon me before I die."

"You must just bear it patiently!
The lord's out hunting, so you see
No-one can enter here but me
Even in dire emergency."

At this, the lady feigns relapse
Leading to deranged collapse.
This puts the beldam in a flap.
She opens up the turret gate
"A priest!
        And pray it's not too late!!
Hurry!!!"

        The chaplain seems to fly
To bring the corpus domini.
Clad in her shape, just as he planned
The knight receives the sacrament,
Drinks from the chalice. Now the priest
Is just as rapidly dismissed
As he arrived. The horrid crone
Bolts the door when he is gone.

The lady lies there with her knight.
I never saw a sweeter sight
Than this charming, lovely pair;
He so handsome, she so fair.
When they had talked enough, and smiled
At dalliance in their private world
The hawk-knight bowed and kissed her hand –
He must return to his own land.
She softly asks him to return
To her as often as he can.

"Lady, when you wish for me –
Within the hour, here shall I be.
Be temperate, and use discretion
Or harm may come. Immoderation
Will cause the dowager's suspicion
And will disclose us. She delights
To sneak and spy by day and night
For evidence to feed her spite.
She will jalouse our tenderness
Run to her brother to express
Every vile detail of her doubt.

"Be sure excess will find you out.
If we're discovered, as I fear,
Through love's sweet folly –
                    Then, my dear,
By spite and malice I'm betrayed
And all my magic powers fade.
I'll die a death I can't evade."

With this, the hawk-prince flies away
Leaving the lady full of joy.
In perfect health, she wakes next day
Remaining cheerful all the week
With fresh bright roses in her cheeks.
Her smiles disclose a charming dimple.
She treats her body as a temple
Her former beauty is restored.
Her manner changes; furthermore,

She is content to stay indoors
Rather than seek elsewhere for leisure.
In privacy is all her pleasure
For then she may invoke her lover
To enjoy their bliss together.

Early and late, by night and day
Soon as her husband is away
She may embrace her handsome knight.
Late and early, day and night
She may speak with her only friend.
Pray that her joy may have no end,
Farewell to all her pain and woe
– May the good Lord grant it so!

And there it is. Her happiness
From each meeting and caress
Changes her demeanour utterly.
Her mean old husband is so sly
That in his heart, he wonders why
His wife should show this sudden change.

His sister is the one to blame!
One day, he goes to quiz the dame
And says
        "I think it mighty strange
To see my wife so well turned out.
Pray tell me how this comes about."

The hag protests she doesn't know –
She's seen nobody come or go.

"Nothing escapes my vigilance
No rash intruder stands a chance!
There is no male friend, or lover.
Just one odd detail of behaviour
Seems rather out of character –
Though once, when left alone, she pined
Now, your lady's more inclined
To want to be alone. No sign

But that."

        "Aha!" the old man cries
"Alone – that comes as no surprise!
Now, do one little thing for me:
When I get up tomorrow, early,
And you have locked and barred the gate
Pretend that you are going out.
Let her lie in.
                And then, you wait
Hidden in some secret place
To spy on her with watchful eyes
To see who comes to call, and where
He comes from, to bring joy to her."

And with this plot, they go their ways.
Alas! A wicked trap is laid
And our true lovers are betrayed.

Three days later, so they say,
The lord pretends to go away:-
"The king has sent for me today
By letter, and I must obey.
But I will soon be home, my dear."

Was ever wretch more insincere?
Off he goes; the door's made fast –
His lady is alone at last!
The dowager creeps off to spy
From behind the tapestry
And out she pokes her prying nose
For all she's hankering to know
About what company she keeps.

In bed, my lady cannot sleep.
She doesn't dream of counting sheep,
But revels in her fantasy
Of the hawk in majesty.
He comes there without hesitation
Or momentary procrastination.

How joyous is their dear reunion
In words and looks their sweet communion
Till time comes for them both to rise
And bid farewell, for he must fly.
The mighty bird takes to the sky.

Now the peeking biddy knows
How the lover comes and goes.
It puts the wind up the old witch
To find out that he is a fetch!
The lady has a paramour
Who casts the fairy spell of glamour
To change his form from hawk to man
And, just as quickly, back again.

Milord returns that self-same day
(He wasn't very far away!)
Off to the old man runs his sister
To tell about this weird shape-shifter
A hawk who is a handsome knight.
This gives the skinflint food for thought.
He quickly formulates a plan
To trap and murder this young man.

He sets his smiths to forge iron bars
Hammer the tips until they're hard
And furnish them with wicked barbs.
They're sharper than the keenest razor.
He fixes them in the embrasure
Through which the lady's lover goes.
They are deployed in close-set rows
Firmly cemented in their place.

Grant the goshawk, God of grace
Foreknowledge of a plot so base!
I pray to the good Lord above us
Shield and guard these guiltless lovers.

In the chill hours before the dawn,
The miser rises with a yawn

And bids them blow the hunting horn.
His miserable sister's rousted
To wave farewell and see them out.
She's hurries crossly back to bed
– There's not a sign of sunrise, yet.

The lady eagerly awaits
The hawk, who is her soul's true mate.
It's time, now that the coast is clear,
To summon him.
                    And when he hears
Her voice, so sweet and gentle, say
"Love, come to me, we have all day"
He leaves at once, without delay.

In his majestic strong-winged flight
He soars up to the window light
  – But there are rows of cruel spikes.
One runs him through.
                    The bright red blood
Gushes in a crimson flood.

When he sees his wound is mortal
He tears free from the cold sharp metal
To dive down, draggled and ungainly
Onto the bed beside the lady.
All the sheets are stained and bloody;
His life pours from the dreadful gash.
The lady is distraught with anguish.

He says to her "My heart's true wife,
In love of you, I give my life.
It is as I foresaw and said –
Your changed demeanour strikes us dead."
At this, she falls in death-like swoon
And, for a while, lies limp and prone.
He gives her kind and gentle comfort –

APSLEY 06

"All our sorrows are as naught
For I foresee you'll bear my infant;
He will prove a noble son –
Your solace, in the time to come.
His name shall be Yonec, and he'll
One day avenge us with his steel
And slay our cruel enemy.
I must not stay, but leave at once."

His wound still gushes blood, unstaunched.
In agony, away he flies
To the sound of her woeful cries.
Then her anguish lends her wings
With a great spring she follows him
Out through the window.
                                      God be praised
That by a miracle, she's saved
From death, for this prodigious leap
Is from a height of twenty feet
Or even more.

                    Dressed in her shift
Barefoot and naked underneath
She makes her way across the heath
Following the trail of blood
That from her lover's wound still flowed
In drips and splashes on the road.
She takes this path for miles, until
She arrives at a green hill.
In this hill, there is a door
All spattered and besmeared with gore.
She can see this much, but no more.
From the bloodstains, she's quite sure
That her true-love has gone before.

So in she runs, distressed and reckless
There is no lightening her darkness
No glimmer penetrates the gloom.
– Pray God that this be not his tomb.

She runs on, headlong down the path
Straighter than an arrow shaft
Dark-hollow as the deepest mine.

She pays no heed to place or time
Until she's passed right through the mound
Into a lovely flowery mead.
But here's a sorry sight indeed –
The grass is wet and blood-bedewed.
The lady, frightened and subdued,
Still follows on with fortitude.

Nearby there stands a city, bounded
By the strong walls that surround it.
Every house, great hall and tower
Seems fashioned of the purest silver.
Above all, the grand rooms of state
Are opulently decorated.

Towards the city lie the marshes
Forests, parkland and fenced pastures
Grazed by well-fed cows and sheep.
The other way leads to the keep
Ringed by a river wide and deep
Many ships have moorings there
– Some three hundred sails or more.

The seaward gates are open wide
Downhill she runs.
                    She is inside
The city, always on the trail
Of the fresh blood upon the ground
Which leads her onward through the town
Up to the castle. No-one speaks
To ask the lady what she seeks.
No man or woman does she meet.

As she runs into the palace
She sees the paving of the terrace
Red with blood. In the first chamber

She finds a knight, sunk deep in slumber.
She doesn't know him.
                              On she steps
Into a chamber grander yet.
Another knight there sleeping lies
Again she cannot recognise
His face.
              So onward through the door
A third room, finer than before,
And there –
              she finds her true-love's bed.
Its posts and rails are purest gold
Its drapes are gorgeous to behold
Their value never could be told;
The chandelier and candles white
Burn constantly by day and night
Cost the gold of a city's vaults.

Soon as our heroine beholds
The knight who lies there, she well knows
Her lover's face. In deep dismay
She falters, and her legs give way.
Across his body, she lies swooning.
He clasps her in his arms, and groaning
Rocks his sweet beloved, keening
In the passion of his yearning.
When the signs of life return
He comforts her, gently and softly:

"Bele amie, pur Deu, merci!
Alez vus en! Fuiez d'ici!
My darling, for God's love, have mercy!
Go now, at once! Leave me, and fly!
Before the day breaks, I must die.
I've little time left. When I go
My citizens will hear and know
And maddened by their grief and woe
Will, if they find you, make you suffer
For the death of their good leader.
They know full well that you're my lover

And by this love, I am brought low.
For your sweet sake, I'm sad and fearful."

"Dearest love" – her voice is tearful –
"I'd rather die now, here, with you
Than go to suffer at the hands
Of my cold and cruel husband.
He will dispatch me without mercy."

The knight consoles his grieving lady
"Here is a ring. Now, guard it safely.
So long as it stays in your keeping
Your husband will be –
                 like one sleeping.
His memory will be wiped clean
As if these things had never been
And every detail he'll forget
Of your confinement in the turret."

Then he bids her take his sword
"I beg you, keep it – on your word
That you'll surrender it to none –
In solemn trust held for our son.
When he's grown to a strong man
With knightly courage and élan,
One saint's day you'll go to worship
With our son Yonec, and his lordship.

"When you come to a stately abbey
There a regal tomb will be.
You'll hear my death described again
And how I was unjustly slain.
There you must give our son his sword
And tell him all that has occurred
How he was born, and how conceived.
What will he do then? You will see."

When she has learned what must be done
He gives his love a splendid gown
Telling her to put it on

To hide her torn and bloody shift.
And then – alas – they've no time left.
She must leave him. Time runs apace.
With ring and sword her only solace
She leaves the town.

A mile or so,
No more, she hears the cries of woe
Rising from the castle walls
The great bells ring their mournful toll.
From her own grief she faints and falls
Four times. When she at last comes round
She walks back to the grassy mound
Enters the tunnel deep and black
And walks straight through, until she's back
In her own land.

* * *

And there she stays
With her husband many days
And years. He makes no accusations
Vile jests or cruel imputations.
A son is born, and all goes well.
He's loved and cherished, and excels
In looks and daring, bravery
Wisdom and generosity.

They name him Yonec. There's no man
His equal in the whole Welsh land.
When he's of age and time is right
They give him armour, dub him knight.
And then there happened, that same year
This strange adventure that you'll hear –
Sit quiet, and prick up your ears!

It is the feast of Saint Aaron
The patron saint of Caërleon
And other cities round about.
Each year, they summon the devout

To join the sacred celebration.
The old lord gets an invitation
He brings his friends, his wife and son
Dressed in the height of wealth and fashion.
Yet – they don't know their destination
As they set out upon their ride.

They have a young lad as their guide
On the straight road they trail the vassal
Until they reach a handsome castle.
In the wide world it has no peer.
There they see, as they draw near
An abbey, with a splendid steeple
Where live many pious people.

The youth finds them accommodation
To wait the morrow's celebration.
In the abbot's private hall
They are made welcome, and dine well.
They hear St. Aaron's mass next day
And then prepare their homeward way.
The abbot comes to bid them stay –
There is so much for them to see.

He himself will show them round
The abbey, which is richly founded.
They must see its refectory
The chapter house and dormitory.
Well, since their inn is satisfactory
And offers lavish hospitality
Milord agrees that they shall stay.

After dinner, that same day
The abbot fetches the seigneur
And party for their guided tour.
First they admire the chapter house
Where there's a grand sarcophagus
Covered with a sumptuous pall
With fine embroidered bands of gold.

At the sides, the head, the feet
Twenty wax candles shed their light
Their sconces are of solid gold
A sight most solemn to behold
That would convert an atheist.
The censer is of amethyst;
In daily ritual, the priests
Honour the dead with sacred scents
Of burning myrrh and frankincense.

His lordship's party is impressed.
They ask the people gathered round –
Who is the man for whom they mourned
Who's buried in such hallowed ground
To take his last and longest sleep?

The citizens begin to weep
And through their tears, they tell the worth
Of the finest knight on earth
The handsomest in all the land
The strongest, fiercest, bravest man
And the most loved.
                    He was their king –
The noblest monarch ever seen.
At Caërwent he met his ruin
A lady's love was his undoing
And, in the end, his passion slew him.

"Since then, we have no lord or king.
We have been waiting ever since
For the arrival of a prince
Who, as he told us, is his son
Of his lady-love begotten."

On hearing this, the lady calls
In a clear voice that's heard by all:-

"Beloved son, now you have heard
How we've been guided by the Lord
Almighty God who brought us here!

It is your father who lies there
Murdered by that ancient lord.
For a long time, I've kept my word.
Now, son, take your father's sword."

In shocked silence, everyone
Hears the mother tell her son
Of his other-worldly father: -
How the two were faithful lovers
How he came to her and made
His magic flight, and was betrayed
By the old man's jealousy;
How he devised and spied upon them
And schemed his fiendish strategem.

Now the truth's told, the lady swoons
Insensible across the tomb.
God has freed her from her pain
She nevermore will speak again
For there, unconscious, as she lies
In her cold collapse, she dies.

Yonec, who sees his mother dead
Swashes off stepfather's head.
The keen sword of his noble father
Avenged the sorrows of his mother.

When these incidents are known
To all the people of the town
In honoured state, as is her right,
The lady, with all sacred rites
Is laid to rest beside her knight.
Then, beside his parents' shrine
They anoint Yonec as their king
And all the bells begin to ring.

This tale was known for many years
And told with mournful sighs and tears
Until, in time, there came the day
The minstrel made this tragic lai

To tell the people of the city
Of the sorrow and the pity
That these true hearts endured for love.

Now they're in paradise above.
The princeling of the silver town
Wears a celestial golden crown
And has, not hawk's, but angel's wings.
She flies beside him, and she sings.

VIII L'AÜSTIC : *The Nightingale*

A story, yes. And here's the way of it –
In Brittany they made this lai of it
Called *L'Aüstic,* if I'm correct,
In the old Breton dialect.
Le russignol, the French would say,
Or *nihtegale* the English way.

The Bretons hold in high renown
The splendours of St Malo Town
As rich and strong as it is pretty.
Two knights were neighbours in this city
And their most noble reputation
Enhanced St Malo's estimation.

One had found a gentle bride
So elegant she took a pride
In dressing in the courtly tone.
The other baron lived alone
A bachelor, whose knightly talents
Outbraved the feats of other gallants,
Admired by all for his prowess.
He gladly gave of his largesse
With open-handed hospitality
Esteemed throughout the principality.

So much he prayed to God above
His neighbour's lady gained his love;
With so much vehemence he wooed,
And all she heard of him was good.
(It's so convenient to adore
The gentleman who lives next door –
He never strays far from your sight.)
She gave her heart with all her might.

So tender was their love, and sweet
And yet so guarded and discreet
They soon became accustomed to

Uninterrupted rendezvous.
They were not spied on or suspected
Since their two houses were connected
Joined from the great hall to the basement.
Except that the lady's private casement
Gave on a wall of dismal stone
Across the garden. This alone
Kept them apart.   And yet she might
While sitting at her chamber light
Talk to her sweetheart. They could pass
Love tokens through the open glass;
Make paper darts of ardent passion.

Their love grew stronger in this fashion
Making the best of ease and leisure
With little to destroy their pleasure.
Except that they could not conspire
Sufficient for their heart's desire
For, when the master rode abroad,
His wife was guarded and immured.
And yet they managed to contrive
Meetings to keep their flame alive.
By day or night they talked alone
Despite the lady's chaperone.

Time passed in dear increase of love.
Come Summer. Every hedgerow, grove
And pasture flourished with new green.
Such apple bloom was never seen.
Thick as the blossom on the bushes
Sweet little birds, larks, wrens and thrushes
Burst into song. Each lusty lover
Thought of his true-love, with no other
End in mind but he must have her.
And so the storm-clouds start to gather.
Likewise the lady's heart must soften
With longing to enjoy more often
His handsome face and manly voice.
More frequent talks would be her choice;
She, with the liveliest cardiac flutterings
Hung upon his every utterance.

So, when the moon shone bright outside
She would slip from her husband's side
While he lay in their bed asleep.
Wrapped in her mantle she would creep
To the high window, lift its latch,
For she well knew her love kept watch
In silent vigil every night.
These lovers took their whole delight
Sustained by this most chaste of graces
– Gazing on one another's faces.

The pitcher visited the well
Too often, and mischance befell.
The patience of her husband broke
Just like the pot of which I spoke.
Night after night she left their bed.
The angriest of words were said,
Over and over he would quiz her
– Just what business took her thither?

"My lord," said the lady, thinking fast,
"There is a joy that has surpassed
All earthly pleasures life can bring.

I love to hear Aüstic sing.
My ears resound with every note
That issues from that sweet bird's throat.
Such is the power of my yearning
I cannot sleep from dusk to morning,
And every night I will rejoice
In the full glory of his voice."

His malice grew with silent vigour
He gave a secret, cruel snigger.
His mind possessed a single thought
The nightingale must soon be caught.
Every bondsman in the palace
Was called upon to serve his malice
Plotting, toiling in connivance
To design a sly contrivance
Some snare or net or cruel trap
All to betray the little chap
Whose singing caused this dreadful worry
And put the household in a flurry.

Down in the orchard something stirred
In chestnut and hazel lurked the bird.
With every twig besmeared with lime
Aüstic was caught in little time
The nightingale was stuck so fast.

They had the seigneur's prey at last
And took it alive for him to see.
Milord, in mad malicious glee
To have the creature in his power,
Went quickly to his lady's bower.

"Come wife!" he called. "Where are you hidden?
Pray come to greet me when you're bidden.
I have him here!" he said with pride,
"Who kept you wakeful, bleary-eyed.
Come. See. I will not be denied.
Now he has got no place to hide
You can sleep soundly by my side."

But when she saw the bird, she cried
And would not be consoled. She raved
Begged that the nightingale be saved:

"Give him to me!" his wife commands.
He wrings its neck with cruel hands
In paroxysmal rage so rough
The little creature's head comes off;
Then, to compound his horrid deeds,
Throws the bird in her lap. It bleeds
Spatters her white chemise with gore.
He turns on his heel. Slams the door.

With grief and terror she's oppressed
Cradles the dead bird to her breast.
She curses with unbridled hate
Traitors who drove him to his fate
Who made the snares to engineer
The death of one she held so dear.

"I'm lost. What shall I do!" she cries.
"Disgraced to fortune and men's eyes
Never again to rise by moonlight
Go to my window-seat at midnight
To see my lover through the curtain.
Alas, I know that one thing's certain
He'll think I'm fickle and despise me.
No wise friend living can advise me.
I'll send poor Aüstic. He'll will prove
The story I must tell my love."

Only the finest samite stuff
Purfled with gold is good enough
Her needlework portrays the bird.
She calls a page, who learns each word.
She wraps the corpse. The page soon bore
The message to her sweetheart's door
And told the story, with sad greetings,
Here was an end to lovers' meetings.
When all the sorry truth was spoken,
Gave him the carcass for a token.

The knight considered every part
And took the tragedy to heart.
Low vengeance had no rhyme nor reason
A knight could never stoop to treason.

He kept his rage within his breast
Sent to a craftsman for a chest: -
A casket to his own design
In every element so fine;
No iron or steel from blacksmiths' forges
But gold and gemstones, rich and gorgeous.

Sealed by its finely fashioned lid
The little nightingale lay hid.

Throughout his life, the shrine was cherished
As nuns revere the holy relics.
On every voyage he took the chest.
The story did not stay suppressed
And grew with telling, till the day
The Breton bard wrote *L'Aüstic's Lai*.

ENVOI

The Moral for the 3rd Millennium:
Lovers are fools, and there's no telling 'em.

Here's my advice to knights and yeomen
Pray keep your mitts off married women.
To husbands:
          be your wives' delight
Keep them preoccupied at night
Or else, beware, some sweeter singer
May put your marriage through the wringer.

Dear ladies, heed. Beware of turds
Who take revenge on little birds
And tear their heads off when they're vexed
For ten to one, it's your turn next.
Lest for your murder they impeach him
Just bugger off, and that'll teach him.

IX MILUN : *The Lai of the Swan*

The teller with a repertoire
Of stories to beguile an hour
Must, by the magic of good verse,
Command attention from the first.
The introduction should have novelty
To emphasise originality –
How tedious if every rhyme
Began with *Once upon a time*.
But, if the author's wit is laudable
And the narrative is plausible
The hearers' pleasure will be audible.
Judicious telling is applaudable.

Here I will begin *Milun*
(Yes, it's the one about the swan –
So many stories feature birds!)
And, with a few well chosen words,
I'll tell you all that I have heard
Of how and why it was composed.
Believe me. I am one who knows.

In Suhtwalès, near Caërleon
Was born our hero, called Milun,
A young man with both brains and brawn.
From the day he was dubbed knight
No one could best him in a fight.
Noble at court, stalwart at war
He was a soldier to the core;
In tournaments, all longed to meet him
But no knight living could unseat him.

He was the most consummate horseman
Whose fame reached Irishmen and Norsemen.
In Logres (England), and far Gotland
In Albany (now known as Scotland)
Were many men who envied him –

And yet no rival could bedim
The honour due to his ability.
He was the toast of the nobility
And kings and princelings loved Milun.

Quite near his home, there lived a baron
A nobleman of great good fame;
Alas, I never knew his name.
This baron had a lovely daughter
With every elegance of court. Her
Heart and mind were captivated
By all the tales that were related
Of Milun's prowess. She sent word,
From the repute that she had heard,
She'd give her love, if he'd permit it.

This was as Milun would have wished it.
He sends his thanks with joy and love –
His heart is hers, by heaven above,
To serve her till his dying day
And never turn aside or stray.

His go-between is richly paid
A pledge of fellowship is made.
"My friend" said he, "Go and discover
Where I may meet my dearest lover
Yet keep our trysting-place discreet.
Pray take this gold ring to my sweet
And tell her this –
                          when she commands,
Send you. I'll come. I'm in her hands."

The messenger returns to her
And tells her what she yearns to hear.
She wears his ring! A joyful dance
To learn that what she wants, he grants.
Outside her room, there's a plantation
Where she may take her recreation.
This is their place of assignation
And Milun's frequent destination.

He comes so often, loves so deeply
That their brief idyll ends completely.
Things, as things will, get out of hand
Her pregnancy is quite unplanned.
When she is sure about the signs
She sends for him, and speaks her mind.

"I've lost my honour and good name
Exchanged a virtuous life for shame.
The law decrees a harsh reward –
Either tormented by the sword
Or to some wild remote country
Be sold in cruel slavery."
(That was the custom in those days
They followed their ancestral ways;
Folk were severer, heretofore,
And did not follow Norman law).

Milun stands by her: "I will do
Whatever you require me to."

"Soon as you can, after the birth,
Send to my sister in the north;
She's married to a wealthy man
A prominent Northumbrian.
My sister's worthy, good and wise
A fountainhead of sage advice.
She'll take my baby in her care
I know he will be happy there.

"Let it be written in a letter
Backed up by spoken word:
                                        – Your sister
Sends this child to your protection
The blameless cause of great affliction.
In duty, bring the babe up well,
Whether it be boy or girl. –

"I'll lace your ring around his throat
And send with it a little note:
The name of his illustrious father
And the misfortunes of his mother.
These are the tokens that will prove
That he is born of our true love.
When he's grown up, and has good sense
And reason in his arguments,
Then he may keep the ring and letter,
And, perhaps, one day, find his father."

This plan they both agreed forthwith
To act for better or for worse.
In due course, time came for the birth.
She told all to her aged nurse
A loyal, trusted, loving goodwife
Who acted as both guard and midwife.
She kept the secret so discreetly
That the whole house was fooled completely,
No word or deed to cause suspicion
Of the young lady's true condition.

The infant was a fine lordling.
Around his neck they laced the ring,
A silken purse, and then the note
Well hidden by his baby-coat.
They laid him gently in his cot
Swathed in a snow-white linen cloth,
A splendid pillow for his head;
On top, to keep him snug abed
They wrapped our baby-bunting in
A cover trimmed with marten-skin.

In the plantation, secretly,
The nursemaid hands Milun his baby.
In turn, Milun entrusts him to
A loyal, hand-picked retinue.

Through many a town they make their way
Stopping seven times a day

To bathe and change him, let him rest,
A nurse to feed him at the breast
And minister to every need.
They were a faithful band indeed.

It's a safe road, and by good fortune
They reach the lady's sister soon.
She takes the infant in her arms
Delighted by his simple charm
Dandles and pets the little thing.
The letter and the signet ring
Will tell her all she needs to know.
Her sister's son! She loves him more
Intensely than she did before;
No doubt she'll keep and cherish him.
The followers who came with him
Are reassured, and can depart
Returning home with thankful hearts.

Back in South Wales, fate decrees
His father, Sir Milun, must leave
To seek his fortune overseas
For he is bound by knightly fee.
It is the soldier's lot to roam;
His lady's fate – to grieve at home.
And worse.

       Her father has betrothed
Her to a rich-as-Croesus lord
Who has a cunning business sense
And wields a deal of influence.
When the girl hears of this calamity
She's driven almost to insanity
By longing for her love, Milun.
Her sins will find her out too soon –
She's had a child, and that's not right.
The poor soul's in a dreadful plight.

"He'll find out on our wedding night!

Alas, alas, what remedy
For such a sorry wretch as me!
Marry a husband! How can I do it?
He'll know at once, when we come to it,
That my virginity's long gone.
How can I lie about my son?
Where are you now, Milun, Milun?
A ruined wife expects no grace
To scrub the kitchens is her place.
I'll live in bondage all my days.

"This dreadful outcome's unforeseen.
I have been living in a dream
That I could marry my Milun
And we could hide what we have done
And live our lives quite free of blame
Never a word of guilt or shame
No scandal-mongers to defame
Our family's distinguished name.

"Live as a dishonoured wife?
No! I'd rather take my life.
Even that solace is denied me
For spies are constantly beside me;
My chamberlains, both young and old,
Have dirty minds, hearts that are cold,
They hate true love and faithfulness
And batten on unhappiness.
How they'd delight in my distress!
No, I must bear what fate awaits me;
Vainly wish that death might take me."
And so, upon her wedding day,
She's given, and then led away.

* * *

Meanwhile, Milun is riding home.
He's feeling mournful and withdrawn
Gives many a doleful sigh and groan
Is lost in soulful desolation;

171

Yet he has this small consolation –
Near to his own estate will dwell
The lady that he loves so well.

A stoical, resourceful man
He settles down to make a plan
To solve his problem:
                Just how can
He send a message to his dear
To tell her that, at last, he's here –
Yet be secure in secrecy
And confidentiality?

He pens the letter, sets his signet.
He has a swan, a cherished pet.
Binding the note around its neck
He hides it in the deep soft plumes.
Then he calls for a trusty groom
To guarantee a swift delivery.

"Hurry!" he says. "Take off your livery!
Disguise yourself, and play this cleverly.
Milady's castle, quick as you can
And carry her this precious swan.
This present is for her alone.
To maid or lackey, give command
That it be given to her hands."

This is no sooner said than done.
Off goes the bearer with the swan
Trotting down the dusty road
With quite an armful for a load.
It's not the easiest of jobs
And soon the man is sweating cobs –
A swan's more awkward than a parcel.

Quick as a flash he's at the castle.
The townsfolk think he's quite an eyeful
He really is a sight to see
But keeps his cool commendably.
Sober, collected, debonair
He saunters by without a care.
The peasants point, joke with their mates
But he swans past them to the gates
As they cat-call "Look at that prat!"
They've never seen such great éclat.
He's over the drawbridge, rat-a-tat-tat
At the main door.

The Messenger is enjoying his disguise. Here, he alternates between quiet, courtly speech and an affected, resonant South Welsh accent – like a rugby commentator.

(Clink of coin).   " (Ahem.) Porter, good man,
I AM A FOWLER, WITH A SWAN.
I SNARED IT IN THE WATER-MEADOWS
BY CAËRLEON.

       "(Hissst!) You're a good fellow.
Do me a favour, please.   *(Clink of more coin.)*

          "I NEED
HER LADYSHIP TO INTERCEDE
AND BE MY SPONSOR AND PROTECTOR.
I KNOW MY PROBLEMS WILL AFFECT HER.
SO MANY THREATS TO ME ARE MADE
I CANNOT CARRY OUT MY TRADE!
I FEAR ARREST AND COURT APPEARANCE

PLEASE GUARANTEE NON-INTERFERENCE.
I SEND THIS SWAN TO BE MY TOKEN."

Porter:
"Friend, none of us has ever spoken
To her. She is kept remote.
Nevertheless, I will find out
If I can find some private spot
That I can take you to. She may
Consent to speak with you today."

The porter's to the great hall, where
A pair of knights sit calmly there
Playing at chess;
                    such concentration
Nothing could break their meditation.
They've no idea what's going on
When porter, messenger and swan
Sneak past the pair on stealthy feet
And creep up to the lady's suite.
He calls her maid to to let them in
And lead them to our heroine.

They make obeisance, and present
The lady with the swan. Her gent-
-leman in waiting's summoned:
"Guard my swan properly.   I'm fond
Of handsome creatures. Give him food.
I'm sure that he will roast up nicely.
I hope the sauce won't be too spicy. "

The messenger is keen and shrewd:
"LADY" he cries, "MY SWAN'S FOR YOU
NO OTHER RECIPIENT WILL DO.
HE IS A GIFT FIT FOR A QUEEN!
A SPLENDID SPECIMEN, WELL-PREENED!!"

He gives the bird into her arms
Madame accepts with grace and charm.
There are things, I don't mind confessing,

A woman can't resist caressing.
She strokes its head, its neck, its throat
There, in soft down, she feels the note.
For sure, this letter's from her lover –
Her blood runs cold, she quakes all over.
The bearer is dismissed, well-paid.

Alone at last! She calls her maid
To help untie the billet-doux
From the swan's neck. The job takes two.
She breaks the seal. There, at the head
His name MILUN is what she read
And kissed a hundred times, and wept,
Before she'd strength to read the rest.
(All you who think "The silly female!"
Have never heard, by post or e-mail,
From a lost love.)

       From first to last
The letter's all about the ghast-
-ly suffering he's going through.
And then –
           he tells her what to do
Begs her to follow what he asks;
His life or death is in her grasp.

This is the substance of her task:-
If she can devise a scheme
Whereby this pair of love's young dreams
May meet and talk, then write it down
Dispatch post haste, via the swan.

"First, you must keep the bird well pent
For three days fasting as for Lent.
Then, when sharp-set, it may be sent
With your note tied around its crop
A cunning airborne letter drop.
A hungry pigeon always goes
Straight to the nesting place it knows.
So, if you love me, darling, send

175

A message by our feathered friend."

Brazen audacity! Such wit!
The lady's most impressed by it
And turns it over in her mind.
The swan's well cared for.
                    Now to find
Some stationery. That's the conundrum.
To us, a ball-point pen is humdrum
The lady's plight should make us think.
She scoured the household for some ink;
You can't imagine what a caper
She went through for a bit of paper.
Somehow, by cunning, skill and judgement,
She got hold of a scrap of parchment
– It took a month to find, at least.

Meanwhile, the swan could drink and feast
In comfort in milady's chamber.
At last, oblivious of danger
The lady takes a quill to write
(A swan's flight-feather, purest white).

She pours her heart out, lovelorn thing,
And seals, inside the note, a ring.
The swan is fasted. Then they tie
Her letter to him, and let fly.
The bird, deprived of provender
Homesick, ravenous and eager,
Flies right back to where he came from.
Straight as a die he finds the town
Looks down, and sees our hero's home.

He lands plumb at Sir Milun's feet.
Our hero's rapture is complete
Words can't describe how his heart sings.
He grasps the good swan's mighty wings
Calls loudly for his austringer –
"Feed this fine swan. Harm not a feather."

He searches the bird's breast and throat
And quickly finds the lady's note;
Reads it from top to foot at speed.
This is a happy day, indeed.
Sheer bliss! Such love is here disclosed
With pretty tokens she enclosed.

"I have no pleasure left but you;
Now, tell me all your feelings, too.
Send it by swan, our secret way."
He answers her without delay.

For twenty years the two sustained
This way of life. By the well-trained
And willing swan, they sent their vows

And all went well. They knew not how
To find another means of contact.
The swan was keeper of their contract.
They fasted him before he flew.
Poor bird, you're thinking.   But he knew
His just reward at journey's end;
In each direction was a friend.

From time to time, an assignation
Gave them fleeting consolation –
For, even under constant watch,
Sly conspiracies may hatch.
No-one is kept so close confined
They can't abscond if they've a mind.

Yes, twenty years this game went on
Between the lovers and their swan.
But all this time –
                    what of their son?
His foster-mother does what's right
When he's of age, she dubs him knight.
He's a fine figure of a man.

She tells him everything she can –
How her own sister is his mother
The thrilling history of his father.
Then, showing him the ring and letter
She tells the lad that his begetter
Is a knight of highest honour
Of such daring, skill and valour
That – in all Christendom – no other
Knight's esteemed like his brave father.

When the good lady's told this tale
(Sufficient, surely, to regale
The soul of a red-blooded male)
The lad sits pensive, then aloud
He speaks his thoughts –
                    "Dear aunt, I'm proud
And glad to be my father's son

And bear the name of FitzMilun."

While, to himself, he starts to ponder
"With noble lineage like this
And such a father as mine is,
I'd be of no account, by thunder,
If I did not seek to exceed
His own repute in daring deeds
And make my name in foreign fields."

He has what's needful for a knight –
The true knight-errant travels light –
Next morning, bids his home farewell.
His foster-mother gives good counsel:
"Do all that may become a knight.
Act with courage for what's right.
Make each encounter a just fight.
Defeat is bad; dishonour's worse."
Then she gives him a bulging purse.

From far Norhumbre he heads down
Till he comes to Suthamptune town.
Soon as he can, he puts to sea
Landing at Barfleur, Normandy
Then makes his way to Brittany.
There he distributes his largesse;
Goes jousting.

                Pathways to success
Are open. Men of influence
And affluence make his acquaintance.
Society goes wild about him
No man on horseback can out-joust him.
He won good money from these fights
Gained from the rich, gave to poor knights
Who, out of love and loyalty,
Joined him, and swore fealty.
He spent with generosity.

He never stayed long in one place

But roamed the world's wide open space
Growing in honour, fame and grace.
The young man's bounteous liberality
Was talked of in the Principality
Of Wales, and England too:
                              A knight
Had left their shores and gone to fight
In lands abroad to make his name;
His courtliness had brought him fame
His splendid valour, great acclaim.
And yet, his name is known to none –
He's always called The Matchless One.

News of this upstart reached Milun.
The bold feats of the knight Sanz Per
Resound in the Welsh warrior's ear.
He's sad, reflecting that while he
Could joust, bear arms, and cross the sea,
No Welsh or English knight should claim
The honours due to Milun's name.

He makes his mind up overnight
Takes sail for Barfleur at first light.
He'll throw the gauntlet down, and fight
In tournament with this young knight.
If Milun, by God's grace, prevails
He'll knock the wind out of his sails.
He's angry, and his blood is up;
If he can beat this boastful fop
Just watch the fellow's fan-base drop!
Milun will put him in his place
And wipe the smirk right off his face.
That is the first aim of Milun.

But when this needle-match is won
He'll seek to find his long-lost son.
He knows the youth has gone abroad
But to what land, and by what road?
He tells his mistress of his plan
And asks her blessing.

Soon the swan
Is winging homeward with a message
Wishing him a speedy passage
Expressing her delight and thanks
That good Sir Milun undertakes
– After he's proved his reputation –
To find their long lost son's location.
She will not stand in Milun's way.

Now he has his love's endorsement
He, with a chosen band of horsemen
In full fig, with fiery destriers,
Is on French soil within five days
En route to Brittany, post-haste.
Milun is welcomed most hospitably
Repaying every kindness lavishly.

He's seen at every joust and tourney
And makes good friends along his journey.
All one winter, so they tell me,
Sir Milun spent in Brittany.
More valiant knights have joined his cohort.
In great estate, château and court
The last grey months of cold are spent
In some dank stone fortress pent
Waiting for the end of Lent.

Now that Passiontide is past
At last they break the solemn fast
And joust again. Ah, joy of joys –
Good sport and fighting for the boys.
All the best knights, as I've heard tell
Foregather at Mont Saint Michel:
There are Fleming knights and Bretons,
Frankish men and doughty Normans –
But scarce an Englishman among them.

Milun arrived there in good time
Almost the first one there, in fact.

His gallantry made quite an impact.
He asked: "Where is this Matchless One?"
Many gladly told Milun
From whence this famous knight had come.
His whereabouts are soon revealed
By arms emblazoned on his shield.

Milun takes time to size him up
"I'll tackle him, the haughty pup!
I'll warrant young Sir Know-It-All
Is shortly riding for a fall.
The Matchless One, indeed? I'll match him
And put a blot on his escutcheon!"

The joust begins, and no exponent
Has far to search for an opponent;
Go to the ranks, and look about,
You'll find a rival for a bout.
It's win or lose, and every man
Can find a knight to take him on.

Now you all ask – "What of Milun?"

I scarcely know where to begin:-
Every bout he fought was won
He earned himself a deal of credit
But young Sanz Per won all the plaudits.
His jousting skill's beyond compare
This tournament can show no peer.

Sir Milun watches his career
Notes his proficiency on horseback
How he spurs onward to attack.
Despite the envious thoughts that tease him
This bonny lad has power to please him.

Down to the horse-lines, there to challenge
The Matchless One, and to arrange
A jousting bout.
                    Milun's first charge is
So ferocious that his lance's
Shaft is splintered. The blow glances –
The Matchless One stays on his mount
To strike, and settle the account.
His blow smites Milun with such force
That he falls headlong from his horse.

What's this that meets the young man's eyes
Makes him step back in shocked surprise?
White hair and beard peep from the visor
Of his brave rival.
                    He chokes back tears.
Unseat a man far gone in years?
In chivalry, it's quite untenable
Thus to bring down a man so venerable.
The Matchless One is racked with shame
He bows his head, accepts the blame.

Seizing the reins, he leads the charger,
Presents him to his rightful owner
Bidding him:
                    "My Lord, please mount!
I'm sorry for this incident –

That a brave noble of your age
Should be subjected to such outrage."
He said it all most ceremoniously.

It could have ended acrimoniously
But this was such a handsome gesture.
If you'd been there, he'd have impressed you.
Milun, unhurt, springs to his feet
His face is beaming with delight
For when the lad returned his charger
He saw the ring upon his finger.
Can such things be?
                                He asks the youth:

"Friend, for God's love, pray answer me in truth –
The name, the rank and title of your father
What is your own name; who is your good mother?
– I must know all of it, for I grow old.
Much have I travell'd in the realms of gold
And many goodly states and kingdoms seen.
I've loved a lady fit to be a queen
And, for her sake, I rode at tilt in France
Where dukes and barons fell before my lance.
No honourable stroke unseated me
Until the day that you, good sir, defeated me
And by that blow, friend, you could have my love
And fellowship for life, by God above."

(Forgive me. Lines describing miracles
Are worthy of two extra syllables.
For narrative, I use tetrameters
– They're not as classy as pentameters.
Only the editors of famous magazines
Pay cash upfront for my Classic Alexandrines.
So far Fal Publications has not found the means.)

"All I know," says the Matchless One
"Is what I'm told. I am the son
Of a great British nobleman
Who, I believe, is called Milun.

I am the love-child of his union
With the daughter of a Welshman.
I was sent to Northumberland
And brought up as a gentleman.
My aunt, good woman, fostered me.
She dearly loved and cherished me
With horse and arms she furnished me
And when I sailed abroad, she blessed me.

"I've lived in France quite long enough
I think it's time that I was off –
I have achieved my youthful aims
And have a yearning to go home.
As soon as I've a berth, I'll sail
Returning once again to Wales.

"I long to know about my father
And his conduct to my mother.
I'll show this signet ring, his crest,
And then I'll tell him all the rest:
I know that he will not reject me
But, with paternal love, protect me.
He'll keep a welcome in the hillside
A place there with him at his fireside."

With joy that I need not describe
– There's no disguising his delight –
Milun leaps up to the young knight
And grasps him firmly by the skirt
Of his heavy chain-mail shirt.

"Praise God! I'm healed of an old wrong!
I swear, my friend, you are my son.
To seek and find you I have toiled.
For you I left my native soil."

Hearing this, the youth alights
Sweetly to kiss the older knight.
Father and son look so serene
Such loving words are passed between –

Each one who saw them piped his eye
For joy and pity they all cry.

When the tournament is over
Milun is last to leave. He lingers
Talking with his son at leisure
To find out what might be his pleasure.
Hospitably, they spend the night
Lodged with a merry band of knights
With revelry and such delights.

While their companions are carousing
And the outside world is drowsing,
Milun tells all to his dear son
Whose mother was the only one
True love of his devoted heart.
Her father tore the pair apart
And, caring only for himself,
Married her off for land and wealth
– A title, too – so that was that.
Her husband was a plutocrat
A baron of the Taffia.

"But I was so in love with her.
I could not get enough of her.
I knew she felt the same for me
So I devised a strategy.
A swan became our go-between
For I could trust no human being
To carry messages unseen."

His son replied "Father, I swear
To see you as a wedded pair.
I'll kill her husband in fair fight
And then you two shall reunite.
There's nothing more that need be said.
A busy day. It's time for bed."

Next day, they set to preparation
For their homeward expedition.

A fond adieu to their French friends;
An easy sail, as if the winds
Conspired to help them on their way.
They take the highway the next day –
The Roman road that goes from Rochester
To Viroconium (or Wroxeter).

No sooner had they set their feet
On the stones of Watling Street
Than fate decrees that they should meet
A man en route for Brittany
Seeking a berth, if he can get any.
This servant's come hotfoot from Wales
With the most opportune of tales:

"From his mistress, I have come
Looking for Milord Milun.
Look you, I find you on the road,
Now I'm unburdened of this load!"
He fumbles for the lady's note.

You won't believe the news she wrote:
"My husband's dead. Please come at once!"
This really is a piece of bunce
Milun has fallen on his feet.
He tells his son.

       Their joy's complete.
They ride for Wales without delay
Meeting no mishap on the way.
Soon they reach the lady's keep
Where they embrace and kiss and weep.
Then, breaking free, my lord Milun
Presents the mother with her son –
"So courtly, handsome, brave and strong!"

Their wedding plans did not take long.
No dire relations to invite
No need for anyone's advice;
Their son alone unites the pair

And they are married then and there.
In love, peace, and prosperity
They live in wedded bliss, praise be.

For their sweet love, and happy fortune
The Bretons wrote this ancient tune;
And I, myself, gladly take pride in it
For your delight, I have transcribed it.

Of the swan, there's no more mention
I'm sure that he deserved a pension
For doing such a faithful job.
Now, sleek and lovely, the fine cob
May live a normal life again
And fly downstream to find his pen
(That is to say, his sweet swan-wife).
Swans, like true lovers, mate for life.

X CHAITIVEL : *Sir Wanhope*

My friends, I hope you're feeling soulful
Lai Chaitivel is dark and doleful.
This stirring tale comes to my mind,
A lai heard once upon a time,
Which I remember word for word.
I'll name the town where it occurred
The circumstance of its creation
Its title and denomination:
The name I know is *Chaitivel.*
Perhaps you've heard some minstrel tell
Four Sorrows or *Les Quatre Dols*
(As it appears on other rolls).

At Nantes in Brittany, there lived
A lady graced by every gift;
Accomplishments of many kinds
Adorned her person and her mind.
Each lusty Breton knight or squire –
If he was worthy of his hire –
Was overwhelmed by deep desire;
The moment he set eyes upon her
Insight and reason were a goner.

How could she love them all alike?
She couldn't tell them "On yer bike!"
The misery of mass dejection
Caused by a summary rejection
Would bring about collective heartbreak –
A risk no prudent girl would take.

A man may safely seek the hand
Of every woman in the land,
Yet she can't spurn one swain who clings
In folly to her apron strings
For he might turn in vengeful spite
Just as a pampered dog may bite.
A lady's scrupulously polite

189

To every poor besotted knight;
She's caring, grateful, generous,
Compassionate, magnanimous.
The love-lorn gentleman who courts
Never hears petulant retorts;
She listens to his anguished pleas
Though inwardly, she yearns for peace.

The belle with whom this story deals
Is under siege by love-appeals
From followers who night and day
Flock round their lovely lady-gay.
To the last man, these lordlings deem
Her worthy of their high esteem;
Among them, four knights-bachelor,
Of Breton chivalry, the fleur.
What were their names?
                I'm not quite sure.

Although but lately come of age,
In their brief time upon the stage
They were outstanding, cut a dash
Gleaming from spurs to sabretache;
Generous, valiant, never flash,
Each one a regular El Cid –
They handsome were, and handsome did.

Each looked on her with eyes of love
And did his level best to prove
His worthiness by splendid deeds
– And fetching any little needs.
Without respite, the young men courted
Ever eager, ever devoted
They put themselves to great exertions
To provide trinkets and diversions.
In his own mind, each one professed
Himself ahead of all the rest
In courtliness and diligence.

The lady, who had great good sense,

Spent solitary hours in pondering
Whatever could she do, and wondering
Which of the four had shown most merit
And could be loved with greatest credit.
Who would it be?
                    She couldn't say
For each was worthy in his way.
Such fine young men (I wish I'd seen them)
And not a pin to choose between them.
Such knightly virtues they possessed
How could she pick which was the best?
Take one good man and discard three?
It made no sense. She let things be.

Sweet and tender words were spoken
All four received some small love token.
Each man knew nothing of the rest
And thought himself the dearest, best
And highest in the lady's favour
By reason of his good behaviour.

At every tournament and muster
When knights contend to win the lustre
Of deeds of gallantry in arms
(Thereby to win their true-love's charms)
They wore her tokens, rings and sleeves,
Her pennons fluttered in the breeze.
Each was her champion for love
And as he fought and toiled and strove
In feats of arms and horsemanship
Hers was the name upon his lips.

With her generous demeanour
She kept them on as her retainers
Till Eastertide again came round:-
"To all chevaliers and counts
A splendid tournament's announced
At Nantes parade ground, in the lists,
To challenge our protagonists."

Knights from nations round are coming:
Frankish lords, Normans and Flemings,
From Brabant, Boulogne and Anjou
Bringing their men and retinue
They hurry in from far and wide.
Knights of the Breton countryside
Are fiercely spoiling for a fight.
They lodge outside the city gate
And there they wait ... and wait ... and wait
Till the official jousts begin.

Tempers get frayed, patience wears thin.
The night before the opening bout
Vicious skirmishing breaks out.
When they hear news of these alarums
Our champion knights are quick to arms.
They send for their supporting forces
While grooms prepare the battle-horses
And harness them. Without delay
Their troops are ready for the fray.

Our heroes ride out on the field
Bright helmets, tunics, banners, shields.
The mob outside are quick to see
And know them by their armoury.
Their banderols and gonfalons
Are recognisable at once
In all the pomp of chivalry
And proud heraldic blazonry.

Four challengers are sent to fight
– Two Flemish and two Hainault knights –
Armed and ready, strong and large
Already spurring to the charge
Eager to take our champions on.

Be sure that each brave Breton knight
Shows no desire for craven flight;
Lance down for action, at full pelt
He picks his rival at the tilt.

They crash together with such force
The challengers are all unhorsed.
Our four don't stop to catch their mounts
But leave them free to run about.

Before the fallen knights they stand
Outnumbered by the armoured band
Who hurl themselves into the rescue.
Mêlée and mayhem soon ensue.
As battle rages to and fro
Their swords deal many a swashing blow.

From her vantage in a turret
The lady sees, with eager spirit,
The exploits of her four young swains
Their noble feats of arms, their gains
Upon the field. All four fight well.
The worthiest? She cannot tell.

Fanfares!
      The tournament begins.
The armies swell, the mêlée thickens.
This is no Sunday gallivant
They rumble like earth-moving plant;
A fighting force in serried ranks
Their hoofbeats pound, their armour clanks
They thunder onward in a phalanx
Like so many rusty Panzer tanks.

Before the gates of Nantes that day
Are tourneys, jousting and sword-play.
The Breton lovers play their parts
With strong right arms and valiant hearts.
Success in passages of arms
Adds glory to a young man's charms.
They ride, and carry all before them –
What woman born would not adore them?

War-fever carries them away
Till at the closing of the day
The four find, to their deep dismay,
That in the heat of battle madness
They are cut off from their companions.
Three are struck down and killed outright
Leaving one gravely injured knight.

There on the field he lies perdu;
His broken body is run through
And bleeding from the cruel blow
Which crippled him and laid him low.
A lance has pierced both thigh and hip
Into his belly, where the tip
Remains protruding through his back.

The men who launched this last attack
Gather to see what they have done
And, conscience-smitten, every one
Succumbs to sorrow and remorse.
The flower of knighthood lies unhorsed.

Such fine upstanding brave young men
When shall they see their like again?

They did not kill them by intent!
They cast their shields down, and lament;
A swelling wail of ululation
You've never heard such perturbation
As they cried out their grief aloud.

Out of the city pours a crowd
Responding to the solemn clamour.
They feel no sense of fear or danger
But mingle with the foreign force
To let emotion run its course.
A throng – they say two thousand souls
Grief for the four unites them all.
As mass emotion overwhelms
They loose the visors from their helms
Pluck out their beards and tear their hair.

The fallen have a fitting bier
For each is laid upon his shield
And, shoulder-high, they leave the field
Carried in sorrow to the city
To their beloved.

　　　　　　　　She weeps in pity
At the misfortune of the four
– Then faints upon the hard, cold floor.
When she revives, still pale and wan
By name she mourns each champion.

"Alas, there is no help for me
No happiness I'll know or see!
Above all things I was desired.
Each knight had virtues I admired.
These men adored me ardently
And I loved all four – equally.
Swifter than eagles, stronger than lions,
Lovely and pleasant in their lives

Alas, how are the mighty fallen.

"I used my woman's wiles to draw them,
Preferred to dally than to choose
One above all, and thus to lose
The others, gaining one for three.
How shallow can a lady be!

"I cannot cover up or lie
A tragedy has come thereby:
Three lie there dead, one gravely hurt.
In the wide world, I have no comfort.
The dead shall have full obsequies.
To this man's wounds I shall bring ease
The best that medicine can give.
I dedicate myself forthwith."

He's carried to his lady's chamber
– For him, that phrase has lost its glamour.
Then she ordains rich preparations
For the funeral oblations
A full and solemn requiem
To show she loved and honoured them.
Arrangements are commensurate:
The three will lie in sombre state
Lovingly readied for the tomb
With silken pall and sable plume.
In a great abbey they shall rest –
May God set them among the blest!

The wounded knight lies in her bower.
She does all things within her power:
Summons the wisest doctors there
Commends him to their tender care
To bring what healing they can give.
He soon regains the will to live.
She often sits beside his bed
His heart is greatly comforted;
Yet still she mourns the other three
And thinks about them tearfully.

After they've dined one summer's night
In conversation with the knight
Remembrance of her grief floods in
She bows her head, her eyes grow dim.
He sees her sit there pensively
And wonders what her woes can be.
With gentle voice, he says:

"My dear.
Why do you brood? Love, I am here
I am a friend you can rely on

Here is a shoulder you can cry on."

The lady, pale and lachrymose
Replies in tones most piteous:

"Good friend. I sat there reminiscing
Of your companions who are missing.
No gentlewoman of my station
– With beauty, grace and education –
Has ever, since the years of yore
(Nor ever shall, of this I'm sure)
Earned the love of such a four
To lose three in one day of war.

"Your own life was so nearly claimed!
You lie there lame, and worse than lamed
Your body permanently maimed.

"Because I loved you all so dearly
I wish to honour you sincerely.
The story I shall set in verse
For future readers to rehearse
This tragedy for evermore
About My Sorrows; they are Four.
I'll name my lai *Les Quatre Dols*.
God's mercy on their noble souls."

It really is a crying shame
That she should choose so crass a name.
Stupidity, or arrogance?
The lady's no Marie de France
This nonsense must be stopped at once.

He cuts in:
           "Write it, by all means.
That fateful day haunts both our dreams.
Some time has passed, and time will heal
The pains that tender ladies feel.
Compose your lai, my dear – and yet
– The title's inappropriate."

What can he say? It's quite a poser.
She's not as clever as Jane Tozer.
She writes the most depressing tomes
Lugubrious mawkish little poems.
He can't tell her her work is drivel.

"For my sake, call it *Chaitivel!*
I am Sir Wanhope, Sir Despair,
Sir Desolate, Sir Full of Care.

"I have good reasons for this name;
To them, all stories are the same.
They've shuffled off this mortal coil
They're buried in good Breton soil.
For your sweet love they pined and languished
By gallant death their pain is vanquished.
A bell commemorates their souls
– Send not to ask for whom it tolls.

"The comrades only lost their lives
My losses cut more deep than knives.
They were struck down in manhood's pride
For love they lived – in hope they died –
One moment's pain – a sudden kill.
While I –
        nurse desires I can't fulfil.

"I only am escaped alone
To tell thee. Lady, hear my moan!
I'm weak and lost in my distress
The captive of my useless flesh
Which suppurates in thigh and groin.
No child shall issue from these loins.
You are the treasure of my life;
If fate were kind, you'd be my wife.

"Dearest, to see you come and go
Adds daily to my weight of woe.
Morning and evening, at your leisure

I can enjoy my only pleasure;
In conversation, face to face
I have the mercy of your grace.
All other joys are out of reach
– Caresses, kisses each to each.
My only solace is in speech.

"You say your sorrows number four;
You cause me, dear, one hundred more.
To die would be a kinder fate
Than love I cannot consummate.
Take heed of these grave words I say
No more *Les Quatre Dols*, I pray.
Le Chaitivel's a fitting name.
Who changes it will be to blame."

"I vow" she says "*Le Chaitivel* –
A lovely name. I like it well."
So they set to that very day
To write their melancholy lai
And taught their bards this tale to tell.
When it was sung, it sounded well.

Some tellers call it *Quatre Dols*
It's *Chaitivel* on Marie's scroll –
It makes no difference, on the whole.
She heard the story in her youth
Each title has the ring of truth
And what you see is what you get.
In Brittany, they sing it yet.

I heard no more about this lai
And so have nothing left to say.
I shall go out to greet the day
May it be full of joy, I pray.

XI CHEVREFOIL : *Withywind*

A pleasure, to my heart and mind,
Is this lai, known as *Withywind.*
I'll tell the truth about who made it,
For whom, and why;
                          who sang and played it.
The young tree in the green wood
Sweet honey in the flower.

I've often heard it told to me,
And read it in some library,
About the ardent love between
Young Tristram and the Cornish Queen .
They loved together, soul to soul,
The two halves of a single whole.
Then bitter sorrow came their way
And death, upon the self-same day.

On Tristram, King Mark bent his ire.
His son-called-nephew, bard and squire,
Loved the young Queen. In punishment
He sent him into banishment.
Back to his home he went, forlorn,
In Suhtwalès, where he was born.
On pain of death, there must he stay.
For a whole year he went away.

He could not bear it; chanced his life
To death, destruction and to strife.
He loved his father-uncle's wife.
Don't think it strange. To love with constancy
Leads to disquiet and despondency
If fate and circumstance conspire
To thwart the way of heart's desire.

Tristram was pensive and depressed
And, leaving Wales, went south and west
To Cornwall, by the quickest route

Avoiding capture and pursuit.
He made a hide in the wild wood
As near the Queen's house as he could,
And skulked alone, well out of sight.

He only ventured out at night
When churches rang the curfew bell.
He broke his cover as dusk fell;
In peasant lodgings laid his head
With humble rustic folk broke bread.
He asked for rumour and report
Of how things stood with king and court;
And thus he heard, from these poor commons
That King Mark had decreed a summons
All knights and barons must report
To great Tintagel, where his court
Would celebrate at Pentecost
The coming of the Holy Ghost,
With banquets, pomp and revelry
In full array and panoply.
And there – the lovely Queen will be.
The young tree in the green wood
Sweet honey in the flower.

Young Tristram's spirits rose to hear
That his true love was coming near–
He knew he couldn't fail to see her.
"The day her cavalcade will ride
I'll go into the wood, and hide;
There's only one route they can take
I'll lie in wait there, for her sake."

He cut himself a hazel stake
Peeled off the bark, cut it four-square,
Exposed the sapwood, pale and bare.
Then, with his knife, he cut his name
TRISTRAM (DRVSTANS, the Cornish say).
"The Queen will pass, and she will see
This tender wand, and think of me."

If Tristram's stave should meet her eyes
She'll notice it and recognise.
He knows, when she should pass that way
The Queen will see and understand
The proud rod upright in the ground
For, once before, he'd used this ruse
A sign that she alone construes.
The young tree in the green wood
Sweet honey in the flower.

They share true lovers' intuition
Communion and precognition.
There will be instant recognition.
His name was all that need be said;
Yet she'll interpret –
                              "Love, I've stayed
Here in the woods for many days,
Waiting and hoping to find ways
To see your face, hear news about you.
I can no longer live without you;
For we are like the withywind
Inextricably entwined
Around this very hazel tree.

"When it is firmly bound in place
And holds the tree in its embrace
The honeysuckle can survive
The hazel bush will grow and thrive.
The young tree in the green wood
Sweet honey in the flower.

"But if some woodsman cruelly tries
To separate them, and to prise
The two apart, the hazel dies
The honeysuckle soon likewise.
Bele amie, si est de nus;
Ne vus sanz mei, ne mei sanz vus!
Dear love, it's like that with us two:
No you sans me, nor me sans you!"

The Queen passed by on a fine horse
To where the trackway took its course
Across a steep bank through the wood;
Just there she saw the hazel-rod
It was his message – just the same! –
With each dear letter of his name.
She knew them all; could understand
The writing of her lover's hand.

She told her escort guards to rein-in:
– She must rest now, her back's complaining
For this is rough and steep terrain.
This clearing is a likely berth
To halt, dismount, loosen the girth,
And answer any calls of nature.
(She's a resourceful little creature
And love is such a cunning teacher.)
– She'll stretch her legs. She called her maid
And left the horsemen in the glade.
She and her faithful Brenguein strayed
A little from the path.

                              She sees
Waiting there beneath the trees
The very man who lives and breathes
For her above all else on earth.
Without her, life is nothing worth.
The young tree in the green wood
Sweet honey in the flower.

Imagine rapture, joy and mirth!
For he can talk with her at leisure
She speaks to him with equal pleasure.
Tenderly they clasp and kiss
In their momentary bliss.

Then she confides her dearest wish –
To bring about, by mediation,
Pardon and reconciliation.
King Mark is smitten with remorse
That anger drove him to enforce
Harsh banishment on Tristram's head
For what malicious tongues had said.

With what rending of the heart-strings
The two resigned themselves to parting!

They wept profusely as she left
And Tristram stood alone, bereft.
He turned to Wales, his native land,
As was his uncle's stern command.

He called to mind their dear embrace,
How he had seen her face to face,
How he inscribed the hazel rod,
All the wise words that she had said.
Tristram, who could sing and play,
Took his sweet harp and made this lai
About the joy they knew that day
That he might nevermore forget.

And so it is remembered yet:-
The young tree in the green wood
Sweet honey in the flower.

Chevrefoil is the French name
In English, *Gotelef* means the same.
This is the lai I've told to you
And every word of it is true.

The honeyed scent of withywind
Always brings it to my mind.

XII ELIDUC : *The Lai of Two Noble Ladies*

This is a very ancient lai
Which I'll retell, as best I may,
Just as I heard it in my youth
And loved its wisdom and its truth.

In Brittany, the bravest gallant,
Virtuous, decent, worthy, valiant
Was Eliduc. A nobly bred
Sweet lady graced his marriage bed.
They had a most contented life
As loyal, loving man and wife
Until the day this famous knight,
To seek his fortune, went to fight.

He journeyed long, he travelled far
Followed his calling to the war,
And set his eyes on a Princess
Child of a King and Queen, no less;
No lovelier girl beneath the sun
Than the exquisite Guilliadun.
Guildelüec, his loyal mate
Still waited at his home estate.

And so they named this *lai bretun*
Guildelüec & Guilliadun.
Yet *Eliduc's* the older name
Those two fine ladies stole his fame.
I love all things traditional
Preferring the original.
So gather round me – you will hear
Of Eliduc the chevalier
The true adventures of this man
And this is how it all began:

Sir Eliduc owed fealty
To the King of Brittany
Who loved him dearly for his loyalty

To people, motherland and royalty.
When the King was called away
This knight, as his lord viceroy,
Did justice well and prudently.
The land thrived in his regency.
Eliduc gained much benefit
Hunted the stag when he saw fit
Followed the hounds from view to kill;
Such horsemanship and forest skill
That the most seasoned verderer
Could find no fault with his seigneur.

But envious gossip starts to brew
About the ambitious parvenu;
Tales of malpractice, false report
Whisper down corridors at court.
Slanderous rumours soon convince
Even his Majesty the prince.
Sir Eliduc is sent away
Summarily. The King won't say
The reasons for his banishment.

The knight is lost in bafflement –
His place at court is fully earned
Yet his reward is to be spurned.
Of what crime is he accused?
A royal audience – refused.
Dejectedly, he rides back home.
In order that the truth be known
He tells his good friends everything
About this peremptory King:

"I was his loyal Knight, none braver
And served the King for love, not favour.
I have committed no offence
Yet they deny me my defence.
Friends, this dismissal is inglorious,
My service being meritorious.

"Sometimes a master with a stick
Bullies his ploughman. Just so fickle
Is a potentate's good grace
Or so the homely proverb says.
Insults and wanton cruelty
Absolve a man from fealty.
I've had enough. I don't enjoy
Being his Highness' whipping-boy.

"He is an upright man indeed
Who serves his King at utmost need
And deals kindly with his neighbour
Asking no reward for labour.
Farewell, my friends. It's time to leave
For Greater Britain over seas
To Logres, where I'll take my ease."

His friends are sad and sick at heart
To hear that he must soon depart.
His wife will govern house and lands
He orders servants, asks his friends
Faithfully to serve and care for her
And keep affairs in good repair for her.
Ending these deliberations
He sets to lavish preparations.

He takes ten horsemen to support him
With wife and servants to escort him.
Guildelüec is quite grief-smitten
To see her husband leave for Britain.
With mutual vows of faith and trust
They part their ways, and go he must
Down to the harbour, out to sea.
He disembarked at Totnes quay.

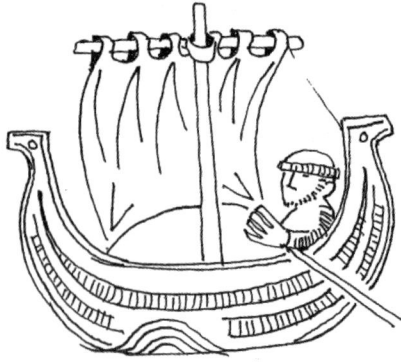

Disputed boundaries embroil
Every inch of British soil.
There's nothing petty chiefs like more
Than a short territorial war.

Near Exeter, in western Britain
Lived a very puissant sovereign
Old, decrepit, white of hair
Without a son to be his heir.
His pretty daughter, fresh and nubile
Was sought in marriage by a noble
Much like her father, full of years –
The nastiest of all his peers.
Naked ambition led to war
Which laid the whole dominion bare.

To save the child from molestation
She is kept in sequestration
In a tower, whose every entry
Is guarded by a well-armed sentry.
Because the stress of war enfeebled
Both army and the common people
The citadel is undermanned
And, fearful that it won't withstand
Prolonged assault, the King decreed
All men must carry arms at need.
Too weak to practice in the grounds
The force was strictly kept in bounds

Forbidden jousting and sword-fighting.

Our hero found the tale exciting
And decided he would settle
In Britain. He had found a battle
That would suit his knightly mettle
– To serve a King he'd never met
Whose little Princess was beset.
Eliduc, our gallant knight,
Felt called to aid them in their plight.

Letters and messages said that he
Would gladly take the old King's fee
And join his loyal armoured band.
For this he'd left his native land.
On condition of safe transit
His troop and he would ride at once. It
Warmed the old King's heart to read
That he had found a friend-in-need;
His state of siege would be relieved.
The messengers were well received.

The King called for his adjutant –
A signed and sealed safe conduct warrant
Was sent post haste to shield the knight,
And all the King's aides expedite
The preparations at the court.
Our hero and his armed escort
Are met with pomp and dignity.
A worthy merchant of the city
Offers lodging in his home
Gladly gives up his grandest room
Hung with splendid tapestry.

Sir Eliduc fares royally
And offers his own hospitality
To soldiers of the principality
Who've suffered hardship in this war
That's left its ugly barren scar.
And still the enemy's besieging

The city and its neighbouring region.
His men are ordered to refrain
From taking any gifts or gain
For the first forty days they serve.
None of the soldiers has the nerve
To flout what he is told to do.

On the third day, they all stand to.
Alarums from the lookout tower
Roused them at the sunrise hour –
The enemy is closing round
Swarming through strategic ground
Intending to surround the town
To storm the gates and break them down.
The populace, in disarray
Begins to clamour in dismay.

Our champion waits to hear no more;
He and his knights prepare for war.
A small company of horse
Makes up the city's full resource,
For many men are hurt or hostage
And cannot join his entourage.
All those who can fight come at once
Without waiting for the summons.
Our hero leaves the sally-port
With fourteen horsemen in support.

"Sir knight!" they cry "We ride with you
And do what we are ordered to."
And he replies
                   "I thank you, friends,
For every man of you intends
To thwart the usurper's vile transgression
And avenge barefaced aggression.
If we engage them here, we might
Rebuff them by defensive fight.
Yet I will gladly hear the man
Who can devise a bolder plan.
We few, by skilful skirmishing,

212

Could overthrow their war-machine."

One man speaks up: "In this 'ere wood
Through coppice runs a narrow road
By which the enemy deploys
Attacks wiv lawless soldier-boys –
Who, when they're done wiv loot and pillage
Return to billets in the village
All nonchalant, like sitting ducks.
Let's 'ave a go and chance our luck.
'Oo knows? They might well come to 'arm
Slouching on 'orseback, 'alf disarmed!"

A daring venture, worth a try,
An honourable way to die
Delivering a mortal blow
To the ambitions of the foe.
Our hero likes this cunning ruse:

"I swear to all of you who choose
To join me in this deadly strife–
He who dares not risk his life
To fame and glory is a stranger.
But he who faces mortal danger
Is loved by every charming beauty.
Now follow me, and do your duty.

"We will retrieve a pile of booty
And every soldier gets his share
Such is the fortune of la guerre.
Do not forget your solemn oath
To serve the King. Men, keep your faith.
I'm with you in this deadly game
And what you do, I'll do the same.
No man of you shall come to harm
While I am standing at his arm.
If there's no loot, a greater prize
Still waits for us. In all men's eyes
We will gain honour for our deed.
We do not fight the foe for greed!

In high morale they march beside him
And through the forest paths they guide him.
While they lurk there, the knight discloses
The strategy that he proposes:
To trap them by an ambuscade
In this dark narrow enfilade.
He sets their ambush by the lane
Until the army comes again
Each man deployed with full instruction
For his part in this destruction.
They would have followed him through hell
"À Eliduc!" their battle yell.

When the invading force appears
That is the cry that meets their ears
As they file through the narrow track

Among the thorns. No going back.
Eliduc bawls out "Attack!"
His men leap from their bivouac
The knight calls on his bold companions
To fight with courage at his summons.

They show no mercy. No-one's spared
Within the compass of the sword.
The foemen, utterly dismayed
To be so cunningly waylaid,
Are routed quicker than a thought.
Captain and many knights are caught,
Disarmed as prisoners alive.
Thirty are trounced by twenty-five
In custody held by the squires.
The valiant band regroups; retires
In jubilant mood towards the fort
In triumph.

        Their bold venture's brought
Rich pickings, armour, gold and horse
And many prisoners to escort
On foot beside the mounted cohort.
The King sees the approaching force
From the vantage of his turret.
The poor old man is sorely worried.
He racks his brain to understand
How this huge armour-wielding band
Could come in full accoutrements.
A fearsome host! The King laments
Believes that Eliduc betrayed
His finest men by way of trade;
A gallant few left with this knight
Yet now an army hove in sight.
No wonder they're not recognised
And good Sir Eliduc's despised.
The King commands "Secure the gate!"
The garrison must lie in wait
With bows and arrows. "Men, be dauntless!"
But soon the King sees this is pointless.

Our champion sends a courier
A squire, who begs his Highness hear
The dashing courage of this knight
Who, with a few men, put to flight
The vicious hirelings of the foe.
The messenger basks in the glow.
No other hero, it's agreed
Has carried off so bold a deed:-
Their captain seized, with twenty-nine
Seasoned soldiers of the line,
A creditably large death toll,
With many wounded on the roll
To crown this day of martial glory.

And when the King has heard the story
He's bursting with relief and joy;
Runs from the tower to greet the boys
And Eliduc, who did their duty.
In thanks, the King gives them the booty
And all the prisoners for ransom.
Eliduc's response is handsome
As befits our noble charmer;
Victors and captives share the armour.
Eliduc takes a small proportion
Three horses are his only portion.

* * *

After this feat of which I sing
Our hero's favoured by the King.
Upon his sacred oath he stands
As Guardian General of the lands
For one year on the royal roster
With all the soldiers he can muster.

So much did Eliduc excel
That very soon the court heard tell
How he was courteous, magnificent,
Manly, noble and munificent.

At this, the Princess can't restrain
Her ardour; calls her chief retainer.

This man of honour and good sense
Presents her Highness' compliments
To Eliduc :
        – She warmly greets him
Tells him how much she longs to meet him.
Would he informally attend
And talk together, friend to friend.
Though she confesses to some doubt:
Why has he never sought her out? –

Eliduc thanks her for this honour
Of course he'll gladly call upon her;
Mounting his fiery destrier
With one attendant, rides away
To pay the Princess all his reverence.
He is announced.

            In proper deference
Sir Eliduc waits to be summoned.
When first he sees her, he's quite stunned.
With unaffected gentleness
He pays her courteous address
And thanks her for her invitation
To this private conversation.
The lovely Guilliadun's serene
Comports herself just like a queen –
She takes his hand, and he is led.
They sit together on a bed
Talk of more things than I can name.

She gazes on his face and frame.
His whole demeanour is so charming
She can find nothing unbecoming
And so admires him in her heart
That she succumbs to Cupid's dart.
The girl is utterly disarmed,
She blanches, sighs and looks alarmed.

Her position's inextricable;
To make things worse, it's inexplicable.
She cannot speak a single word
For fear that he will think her forward.

They spend a pleasant while together.
She craves for longer time. However,
She gives him her reluctant leave,
Although inwardly she grieves.
He rides home sadly, with head bowed
And downcast heart. He thinks aloud:

"Such innocence, such youth and beauty!
Child of the King, to whom my duty's
Sworn in honour. The Princess
Conversed with such sweet gentleness.
She breathed profound and tender sighs.
The gods of fortune must despise
Me. Though I've spent some time at court
I've never seen her; gave no thought
To meet Guilliadun face to face…"

At this he paused, and prayed for grace,
Thought of Guildelüec his wife
"I swore to her, by soul and life,
Devoted constancy and faith.
So much for loyalty and truth!"

The girl he left not long ago,
Desires to have him as her beau.
She's never met so fine a man;
She'll try to keep him if she can.
Waking dreams churn in her head
She lies there restless in her bed
All night she fidgets without sleeping
Her pillow moist with silent weeping.
First love, the all-engulfing feeling
Leaves a mark beyond all healing.
Only a spirit mean and poor
Disdains the impulse to adore.

She rises at the skylark hour
Calls from the window of her bower
Her steward comes to her apartment
To learn of her predicament.

"Alas!" she says "Nothing goes right!
I'm in a wretched, sorry plight.
I love the King's new Knight Commander –
He is a second Alexander.
I cannot sleep or close my eyes,
No, not one wink. It's no surprise
After a night spent sad and restless
I woke this morning pale and listless.

"If Eliduc shares my emotion
And he will swear his true devotion
I'll be the cat that got the cream!
While he'll fulfil his wildest dream
He will gain influence and power
With throne and kingdom for his dower.
He is so cultured, good and wise
That if I'm nothing in his eyes
And he can't love me in return
Then – farewell life! I'll grieve and yearn
And pine away."
                    Her frank disclosure
Caused the poor steward discomposure
But this loyal, caring man
Gives her the best advice he can:

"Lady, your heart is sore, not broken.
Dear, if you love him, send a token,
A message with some dainty thing –
A girdle, ribbon, or a ring
That he can wear, and think of you
And the great honour you bestow.
There is no emperor on earth
Too proud to recognise your worth
Who'd not receive your love with pleasure.
You are this Kingdom's greatest treasure."

The Princess hears him, and replies:
"How shall I see with my own eyes
Whether my gift is well received
And his esteem's to be believed?
I've never met a courtier
Who would not keep, without demur,
Whatever gift one might deliver,
Whether he love or hate the giver.

"He might seem kind, but slyly mock;
I'd hate to be his laughing stock.
Yet nonetheless we may well trace
His secret feelings in his face.
These are wise words that you have spoken.
I will send Eliduc my token.
Go, trusted friend, you must prepare
To be my secret courier."

"I'm ready, child, before you ask
To undertake your every task."

"Take him this ring of precious gold
And this silk sash. These favours hold
A thousand greetings from my heart."

She lets her Chamberlain depart.
Almost recalls him. (She's inclined
Quite frequently to change her mind –
Like most princesses, you will find.)
Lamentingly, she stays behind.

"Alas! My poor heart is in danger
From this handsome wandering stranger.
Is he in truth a well-born knight
Or just a fickle fly-by-night
Who may as suddenly depart
And leave me with a broken heart?

"I'm acting in a foolish way;

I only met him yesterday
And now I offer him my love.
Oh, what if he should disapprove!
Yet if he's noble, he'll be kind.
I've made my choice.   What will I find?
For if he can't return my care
I shall be stricken with despair
And nevermore find joy in living."

While she sobbed in deep misgiving
Her servant ran in utmost haste
To Eliduc's own lodging-place,
Saying that the Princess sent him
With little favours to present him -
A ring and girdle, which the knight
Received with obvious delight.
He slipped the ring onto his hand,
And with a twist he neatly spanned
His waist with the smart silken belt,
In gratitude so clearly felt
That neither one spoke any further;
Except that Eliduc asked whether
The man would take some recompense.
This was refused, without offence.

*Forgive me, please, if I digress, while he runs home to
his Princess. I find it tricky to explain the function of this
Chamberlain. Meaning becomes obscured by time – and it's
a lousy word to rhyme! I think our Princess would disdain
a common wrinkled old retainer. Instead she treats him an
ally. Their conversation gets quite pally. He doesn't treat her
with due worship, but sits down to a good old gossip; jollies
her with gentle kidding, then rushes off to do her bidding – at
every whim, however weird. He's nothing like a wizened
greybeard, but young and bright. It's set me wondering. No
wise old King would be so blundering as to entrust his virgin
daughter to a young swain. Lamb to the slaughter springs to
mind.*

Surreptitious amorous fumbling would set the royal fury

rumbling in thunderclaps about his head. Yet this man visits
her in bed! His feet are fixed under her table, just like a
eunuch in the fables told by the Princess Scherezade. There is
no need to set a guard. He's master of the situation, without
some horrid mutilation to curb his lustful, youthful appetites.
I think his tastes incline quite otherwise. I've no doubt that he
loves her dearly, but this regard's platonic, merely; a faithful
buddy, always there for her, he probably can style her hair
for her. His company is blithe and gay, and you can take that
either way. In short, in vulgar modern parlance, he's camp as
lamé jousting tents. They have each other's confidence, and
empathy with shared experience. Like him, she's an oppressed
minority, subject to patriarchs' authority. Of such are lifelong
friendships made. The Princess finds her loyal aide and
servitor a paragon. Now, revenons à nos moutons.

So, without more ado –
    The groom
Returned to his Princess's room.
"Madam, he thanks you graciously."
She interrupts rapaciously:
"Don't be so coy! Just tell me straight –
DOES HE LOVE ME? I can't wait!"

"I'm certain," says her wise advisor,
"That Eliduc's no womaniser.
He has discretion, I believe
His heart's not worn upon his sleeve.
It was a simple, manly meeting.
He took the favours, with your greeting,
Elegantly tied the sash
Then put the ring on. How it flashed!
That's all he said and did, my dove."

"He did not think them gifts of love!
And now I've made myself look cheap..."

"Dear heart, I hate to see you weep."

"Oh, he must think me such a fool!"

"By no means, Princess. Please keep cool.
Listen to what I have to tell you.
If Eliduc did not think well of you
He'd have returned your gifts at once."

"Don't trifle with your mistress, dunce!
I know he feels no loathing for me.
I've never hurt or harmed him. Surely
To love a good man is no fault.
If he regards my love as insult
And thinks of his Princess with hate –
He's a miserable ingrate
Deserving death and bitter shame
For treating me with unjust blame.

"I'll never speak of him again
To you, or anyone; nor deign
To ask Sir Eliduc for favour.
So he shall learn from my behaviour
How love has left me quite distraught.
Yet he may not stay long at court
To see the misery he's caused."
And with a bitter sigh, she paused.

"My lady has no need to fear–
He must remain here for a year.
He swore the King, by knightly warranty,
To serve him loyally. I guarantee
That if it is your Highness pleasure
You can tell everything, at leisure."

She's over moon and stars to hear
That Eliduc must stay a year.
The naïve girl can have no notion
Of the tumultuous mixed emotion
That stirs the bosom of the knight,
Or that he loved her at first sight.
He knows no pleasure or delight
But thinking of her day and night.

His conscience stabs him like a knife:
What of the vows he made his wife?
He swore most faithfully to love her
And never fall for any other,
When he left Brittany for Logres.
Think of the duty that he owes her.
Is he a husband, or an ogre;
A trusty knight, or heartless rover?

He does not want to hurt his wife
But cannot, for his very life,
Refrain from loving the Princess.
He longs to enfold her and caress
Her every time their glances meet.
She is so lovely, young and sweet.
Whenever they are face to face
They talk together, kiss, embrace.

He cannot set his heart upon her
Without courting grave dishonour.
He gave Guildelüec his troth
And swore the King a sacred oath.
Riven by divided loyalty
To sweetheart, wife, and knightly fealty
He mounts his horse without delay,
And with his squadron rides straightway
With pennons flying, to the tower
To talk with the King, and see his flower.

It was just past the dining hour
The King was in his daughter's bower
With a wise, well-travelled lord, who
Sat with Guilliadun at the board
So as to tutor the Princess
In all the finer points of chess.

The King receives him heartily:
"Come, Eliduc, and sit by me!
Child, you must become acquainted

With this man of pure untainted
Chivalry. This knight is fearless.
Among five hundred, he is peerless."

The Princess is amazed to hear
His praise so fulsome and sincere.
Happy to obey her father
She goes to Eliduc.
                    Together
Snug in a corner, set apart,
Struck dumb by yearnings of the heart.
Fair Guilliadun is terrified
And Eliduc is quite tongue-tied
For love has set them both adrift.
He shyly thanks her for her gift –
"I like it more than any thing."

"I'm glad to see you wear my ring,
Happy that I was bold to send a
Token of my heart's surrender.
Each time this girdle binds your frame
Believe that I would do the same –
Enwrap your waist in silken fashion
Like this, the emblem of my passion.
I love you as I love my life
Long to embrace you as your wife –
If I can't have you always by me
No man on earth can satisfy me.
Eliduc, what shall I do?"

"I'm honoured to be loved by you
It's far beyond my wildest dream
To be so high in the esteem
Of such a wise and noble beauty;
To serve you is my constant duty.
I'll lock up in my memory
The gracious things you've said to me.

"And yet we must remember, dear,
That time is short for us. I fear

I may not stay much longer here
Than to serve the King a year
Or the duration of the war.
According to the oath I swore
I must return to Brittany
For home is where I ought to be,
If you'll be brave, and let me part."

The girl said "Thank you, dearest heart!
You are so courteous, and wise.
How my unworldly trust relies
On your life of experience.
You will anticipate events
And know just what is to be done
About your sweetheart Guilliadun."

Assured of mutual adoration,
They speak no more on this occasion.
The knight rides homeward to his billet
Glad to think of how his skill
At battle tactics won her heart.
They need not spend much time apart,
For he can often see his lover
Enjoy their private talks together,
And love grows daily more and more.

Meanwhile, he prosecutes the war.
Before too long his troops detain
The wretch who caused the whole campaign
By such gross overweening pride –
Claiming the Princess for his bride.
Eliduc frees the countryside;
He's celebrated far and wide
For his prowess and audacity,
Munificence and great sagacity.

* * *

Alas for Eliduc the lover
His tour of duty is now over.

A stronger duty now attaches to him
The Breton King sends three dispatches to him
To tell him that his native soil
Is ravaged, barren and despoiled;
All its castles have been razed
And the whole nation is laid waste.

The King is sorry, full of woe
That he'd let his commander go.
He had heard prejudiced advice
And looked on truth with jaundiced eyes.
Of all these treacherous accusers,
Troublemakers and abusers –
Every one who is suspected
Has been forcibly ejected
In exile evermore to languish
For causing universal anguish.

Now in his hour of greatest need
The King requires a friend in deed
Reminds our hero of his vow
And begs him not to fail him now,
But to return with all due urgency.
This is a national emergency.

Eliduc hears these reports,
Yet still the Princess haunts his thoughts.
He loves her with intensity
And her response is plain to see.
Between them both there is no fickleness
Folly, dishonour, lust or recklessness.
Such is their virtue and discretion
That their love finds full expression
In gracious courtship, quiet speech,
And costly presents each to each.
These are their joys as loving friends.

The Princess hopes, and she intends
Him for her partner throughout life.
She does not know he has a wife.

"Alas" says he "I have done wrong
I've stayed in Logres far too long!
I curse the day I saw this place
For here, I saw her lovely face –
Guilliadun, the fair Princess
Who is my soul's true happiness.
She has given me her heart.
When circumstance tears us apart
We're for the dark, my love and I,
For one, or both, will surely die.

"Yet nonetheless, I needs must leave
My honour grants me no reprieve
The King's dispatches are most urgent
And my oath to him is cogent
As is my duty to my wife.

"I must be careful. On my life
I can't stay here, I have to go.
I cannot marry her; I know
The church would never grant us blessing.
Farewell, too dear for my possessing,
For nevermore we lovers meet.
Parting's sorrow is not sweet.
Gentlefolk will think me shameworthy,
Yet, to my love, I'll not be blameworthy.
Her dearest wish will be my guide
I'll follow what she may decide.

"My lord the King needs me no more,
Now there's no longer threat of war.
My liege-lord summons me away;
I'll ask for leave before the day
My tour of duty here expires.
I'll ask my love what she desires
When I have told her all my plight;
She's sure to know just what is right.
I'll do whatever's in my power."

His mind made up, seizing the hour
He asks the King for leave to go;
Reading the letters out, to show
His seigneur's urgent call for aid
A summons that must be obeyed.
Her father sees what ties constrain him
And knows no power can detain him.

The King, distraught in heart and mind
Offers him gold to stay behind.
"Eliduc, choose, from all my treasure,
Whatever goods may be your pleasure
One third the realm – yours to command
If you stay here as my right hand
To be co-regent of the nation
In lifelong mutual obligation."

"By God" he says "I can't accept,
Or live to know my sword-arm slept
When any knight of worth would speed
To serve his liege in time of need.
His envoys came to summon me
Far over land and over sea.
If danger threatens your domain
Send for me, Sire, I'll come again
With a strong force of fighting men.
My lord, I shall not fail you then
But gladly do what's in my power
To serve you in your darkest hour."

The King thanks him for this support
And gives him leave to quit the court.
In gratitude, his Highness proffers
The contents of the kingdom's coffers.
The royal bounty knows no bounds –
Fine gold and silver, horses, hounds,
Silk robes and hangings, costly, splendid
A fair reward for service ended.

Our hero takes a modest share

And asks his Highness fair and square
If he may speak with the Princess.
The King most willingly says "Yes"
He sends a page to go before
And open wide the chamber door:
"Your champion to see you, mistress."

She greets him with six thousand kisses
And calls him everything endearing.
Alas, his news is far from cheering.
He briefly brings her up to date
For her advice will seal his fate.

Before he's finished with the tale
And said farewell, she's deathly pale
Consumed by grief, she crumples, senseless
Falls before him, quite defenceless.
The knight begins to rave and weep
To see her narcoleptic sleep;
Kisses her lips and holds her close
Till she's no longer comatose.

When she revives, he says:
                    "My dear
There's something I must beg you hear.
You are my life. You are my death.
You are the reason I draw breath,
My joy and comfort. Sweetest friend,
On your advice my hopes depend
For all the faith that is between us.
Your judgement has no streak of meanness
Your woman's heart is full of pity.

"Sweetheart, I must leave this city
Farewell to England, love and beauty,
For I am called to do my duty.
I've made my adieu to the King.
I pledge, whatever fate may bring,
To trust my future to your pleasure.
Destiny's not ours to measure."

"Let me come with you. I will follow.
Here, without you, life is hollow!
If you won't take me, I've decided
To kill myself. I can't abide it
Life without joy or benefit;
Better make a peaceful end of it."

He speaks to her of love; the balm
To bring her troubled spirit calm.
He comforts her as best he might:

"My sweet, I am your father's knight.
If I take you, I'll be forsworn
And hold my loyal oath in scorn;
My pledge to him must run its course.
I swear to you, with equal force,
This solemn, and most binding vow,
That if you let me leave you now
I will return.
     Just name the day.
I'll come to you without delay –
No obstacle can bar my way.
We'll be together, come what may,
Unless I come to deadly harm.
You hold my whole life in your palm."

She, with a brave and loving heart,
Gives him her blessing to depart
And sets the term, and names the date
When he'll return to claim his mate.
Her champion rises to depart;
Alas, the ache in each fond heart.
Exchanging rings, the two embrace –
Each tastes tears on the other's face.

He leaves the dearest thing on earth.
From Totnes, where his ship is berthed
He's off to sea to join his lord
With horse and armour stowed aboard.
Fair stood the wind for Brittany.

They make good speed to shore, where he
Hastes to the court to see his master
Who greets him joyously. In rapture
Our hero's family, friends and all
Foregather in their master's hall.
But most of all, his wife's vivacious,
A lady lovely, wise and gracious.

Yet he remains cast down in thought
His heart is left at Logres court;
Despite his efforts at good grace
He can't put on a cheerful face.
There is no joy left to express
Till he rejoins his fair Princess
So his behaviour's dull and furtive.

His wife, who's not the least assertive,
Is heartsick at his stern rigidity
And emotional frigidity.
She grieves alone, laments his coldness.
At last she summons up her boldness
To ask – if his affections wander.
Perhaps he had heard some wicked slander
While he was soldiering abroad.
She's never sinned against her lord
And will defend her reputation.
Truth will vanquish defamation.

"Lady, nobody accuses you,
Or maligns you and abuses you.
No – my mind revolves in thought
Of matters at the Logres court:
I promised to their King and sire
That I would come should he require.
I've broken this most solemn vow
He has great need of me just now.

"I pray upon my bended knees
That Brittany should be at peace.
Once the position here is stronger
I'll linger here not one week longer
But sail forthwith to fight for truth.
Until I have fulfilled my oath
I am in torment and I yearn
To make an honourable return.
To break a vow is profanation."

His wife accepts this explanation.
The knight rides off to see his liege
Commands his men to break the siege.
Wise tactics and his strong right arm
Will save the land from further harm.

Before long, time begins to press;
The date proposed by the Princess
For his return, comes on apace.
Now he resolves to sue for peace
And binds the enemy by treaty.
Now he can heed his heart's entreaty
And sail for Logres once again.

Last time he took a baggage train
And a full platoon of lancers
On their richly harnessed prancers.
Now, a few trusted men and squires
Are all the cohort he requires: -
Two nephews (thrilled at this adventure)

His squires (bound to him by indenture)
And our old friend the Chamberlain
(Their confidant and go-between).

Such is the force of love's obsession
They're sworn to silence and discretion
Not to speak one single word
Of anything they've seen or heard;
But quell what rumours noise abroad
Of any thing that's untoward
Concerning him while they're away.

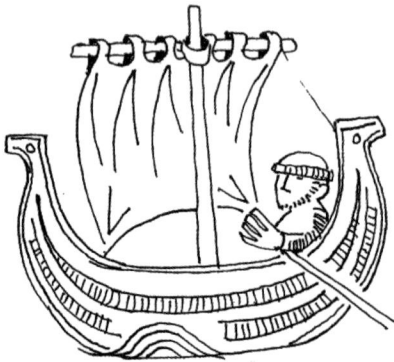

So they embark without delay
And swiftly reach the British coast
The land where he's desired the most.
Wise Eliduc elects to stay
In lodgings several miles away
From Totnes harbour's prying eyes
Lest someone see and recognise
The Breton knight of glorious fame
And seek him out, and spread his name.

He calls the Chamberlain to send
This message to his darling friend:-
Her love, to honour his engagement
Is here according to arrangement
For this is their appointed date.
Now she must leave the city gate

At night, in darkness, secretly
To where her champion will be.
She'll have the Chamberlain escort her
And she must do just as he's taught her.

So walking briskly, but unhurried
Lest he look furtive, sly and flurried
The Chamberlain went on his mission
In plain clothes, not to cause suspicion;
To Exeter, that handsome city,
Where stays the Princess, sweet and pretty.
He asks around, learns by deducement
And offers generous inducements
To meet her in her grand apartments.

Imagine how her girlish heart went
Pit-a-pat to hear his greeting
Promising true-lovers' meeting.
Tears of sorrow and dismay
Quickly evaporate away
To be replaced by tears of joy
And kisses for her serving-boy.

"Princess, compose yourself, and hearken!
As soon as evening shadows darken
You must leave here, and follow me.
We've laid our plans most carefully
To cover each contingency..."

All day, till nightfall, he and she
Study each detail of their route
And when the night-bird starts to hoot
Out from the city, dark and shady
Steal the Chamberlain and lady;
Like flitting owls, the birds have flown.
The pair of them escape alone
Yet she's afraid their plans are known.
She covers up her best silk gown
With rich gold stitch-work on its yoke
With a drab-coloured riding cloak.

An arrow's flight outside the gates
By a dark wood, set among pasture
Eliduc eagerly awaits
The Princess, his inamorata;
When he hears footsteps on the track
He leaps down from his horse's back
Clasps and kisses her in rapture.

Yet, mindful of the risk of capture,
Bids her at once to mount and ride
While he as quickly leaps astride
Gathers her reins to lead her horse.
Swiftly to Totnes run their coursers
Never a stumble nor a slip
Down to the harbour and their ship.
Apart from his small retinue,
The trusty captain and his crew
(No spies or stowaways), there's none
Who has seen him with Guilliadun
Or knows about their flight together.

A steady wind and settled weather.
They make the crossing with great ease
Till close to home, the pleasant breeze
Veers suddenly, and with a roar
Drives them at speed away from shore
Far from the shelter of the haven.
Her rudder breaks, her mast is riven
The rigging tangled, mainsail torn,
All hope of rescue seems forlorn.

Amid this wild and storm-lashed ocean
Each soul prayed with great devotion.
They made their desperate complaint
To Clement, martyr, sailors' saint
And to St Nicholas, their patron:

"Most holy Mary, maid and matron,
Star of the sea, pray intercede:

May your son hear us in our need,
Uphold us in his gentle hand
And bring us safely home to land."

For several hours the helpless boat
Miraculously stays afloat.
This way and that, with pitch and yaw,
She's blown about along the shore;
Each moment they may come to grief
On some bleak beach or sunken reef.

One of his sailors roars and raves
His voice is heard above the waves –
"Pray on, you fools! What are we doing?
Someone aboard has brought us ruin
So we shall never reach dry ground!
And where's this Jonah to be found?
Sir knight, you have a loyal wife,
And yet, at peril of your life,
You've brought your lover, mistress, whore,
Against God and his sacred law
Against all faith and decency.
Let's fling the witch into the sea –
Then we'll have nothing more to fear!"

The Princess cannot help but hear.
Crazy with rage, the gallant knight
Can't leave his true-love in this plight:
"I won't abandon her, you varlet
Misbegotten on a harlot!
Or else you'd pay for each foul word
You filthy, loathsome, treacherous turd."

Our hero puts his arms around her
Alas, what miseries confound her!
Wretched and sick from mal de mer
But most of all distressed to hear
That Eliduc, love of her life,
Is married to a faithful wife
And all this time, she'd never known.

Speechless with shock, she gives one groan
Collapses headlong on the deck
The colour drains from face and neck.
She lies there prostrate, pale and rigid
Extremities quite numb and frigid
No sign of movement, not one breath,
All the appearances of death.

He brought her to this stormy ocean,
Now she lies swooning, without motion.
Poor Eliduc, in great dismay
Is sure his love has passed away.
As the vessel veers and broaches
He wallows in his self-reproaches.

Sorrow and guilt drive him near mad.
Leaping to face the sailor lad
He grabs an oar.
        "I'll kill you, poxy
Spawn of a common quayside doxy!"
One jarring blow, and scurvy Jack
Is toppled senseless on his back.
Scorning to touch the dirty knave
But spurning with his foot, he gave
One kick into a surging wave.
Jack drops, unshriven, to his grave
His body drifts far out of sight.

Deep misery engulfs the knight.
His love lies dead! He is her killer!
Numb with distress, he takes the tiller.
In tragedy, some people find
A superhuman strength of mind;
Great shock and grief lend us some power
To guide us through our darkest hour.
Survival instinct is awoken
Even when the heart is broken.

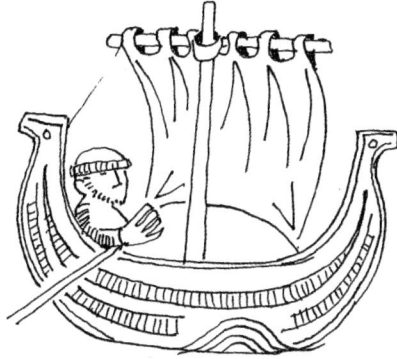

Though anguish almost overwhelms him
Eliduc's a skilful helmsman
Somehow contrives a jury-rig
Enough to tame the drifting brig
And gather enough steerage way
To sail the ship and save the day.
The tempest wind abates its rage
Just as they reach their anchorage
They drop the gangway, make her fast,
And thank their God the peril's passed.

The Princess lies there, like one dead,
As heavy, grey and cold as lead.
Her lover mourns aloud. He'd rather
Fate allowed him to die with her.
He gathers his companions round:-

"Do you know of some hallowed ground
Or sacred spot where we might take her?
I can't abandon or forsake her.
With every pomp and solemn rite
We'll bury her, as is her right,
In honour as a royal daughter.
There, in the place to which I've brought her
She'll lie at peace in God's own acre.
We will commend her to her maker."

His friends, exhausted, sad and spent
Had no advice to give. He bent
His mind and memory to recall
A place.
       "Not far from my own hall
(We can be there before night fall)
In the old woodlands that surround
My house and farms, the hunting ground
A forest, thirty leagues around.
I live nearby, close to the sea.

"There her interment site shall be.
In this calm place – I know it well –
There dwells a hermit in his cell
An oratory for private prayer.
Friends, I've often met him there.
His high vocation is to live
The life of a contemplative,
For forty years he's served the deity
In isolation from the laity."

There, in the chapel, says the knight,
He'll ask the holy anchorite
To bury the Princess. "I'll vow
To do full penance, and endow
The church with land and an annuity
To found a celibate community:
Monks, canons, nuns, in perpetuity
To pray her soul's eternal rest.
May Jesus take her to his breast."

He calls upon his men to swear
To silence on this sad affair;
They will say nothing of the matter.
Then, to the sound of iron-shod clatter,
They head off down the forest track.
He lifts her on his horse's back;
She lies across his saddle-bow
And rides before him as they go.
The bitter tears start to flow.

They reach the wood the fastest way
Find the monk's cell without delay.
But there, they find to their dismay
– No matter how they knock and call –
That there is no-one there at all.
No hermit-friar, or other mortal,
Replies or opens up the portal.

One tries the latch, and he is shocked
To find the chapel door unlocked.
They find a grave with new-turned sod:
The saintly priest was called to God
And died but eight short days ago.
This adds weight to our hero's woe.

The squires go searching for a space
To dig her final resting-place.
Sir Eliduc sternly recalls them.
Their indecent haste appals him:

"We can't inter her in this oratory
Till I consult the high consistory,
And undertake some wise research
On how to build the abbey church
Whose noble, lofty walls will grace her.
Now, by the altar, we will place her
To lie here in the sanctuary.
God's mercy on my fair lady."

With their own cloaks they make a bed
On which to rest her lovely head,
And there they lay her out for dead.
But, as they're on the point of leaving
He holds her in a last embrace,
His brave heart fit to burst from grieving,
He kisses her sweet eyes and face:

"May God forbid that in this life
I should again bear arms in strife,

Or hold myself of any worth
On this miserable earth.
Sorry the day you saw me, dear!
Alas that you should follow here!
You were most fit to be a queen,
Wise, lovely, gracious and serene
And were so soon to claim your throne,
But for your bond to me alone.
You loved in honour, truth and faith
And I have brought you to your death.

"This sin I grievously repent,
And on the day of your descent
Into your grave, I'll join the friars.
This is the fate my soul desires –
To be your beadsman all my days
Who kneels beside your tomb, and prays."

They lock the chapel door, and ride,
Leaving her body safe inside.
He sends a squire ahead to say
The master will be home that day,
And tell his wife that he needs rest,
For he is weary and distressed.

Overjoyed that he's returning,
She welcomes him with home-fires burning
Greeting him with due devotion;
But he returns her no emotion.
She's lived in patience all this while
And gets cold comfort, not a smile
Or kindly word in her direction,
No marks of marital affection.
She dare not ask him to explain.

For two days only he'll remain.
On the morning of next day,
He attends mass, then rides away
Taking a woodland path he knows,
And to the chapel quickly goes

Where his love takes her last repose
And lies there dead, or comatose.

Her pure complexion, white and rose,
Though pale, miraculously shows
No sign that flesh must decompose.
No fleeting breath does she exhale
There are no signs of life at all.
Copious tears begin to roll
As he prays for his true-love's soul.
And when at last his prayers subside
He leaves to take the homeward ride.

Daily, he makes this pilgrimage
To see her at the hermitage.
Guildelüec still wonders why,
So she decides to send a spy
Promising great wealth thereby.
She tells a serving man to try
To follow every twist and turn,
At a safe distance. If he learns
The destination, he will earn
Armour and horse. A fine reward! Her
Servant carries out this order.

Unseen, he follows Eliduc
Noting the pathways that he took
Through the thick forest to the cell.
He watches carefully and well
How Eliduc bows through the entry,
With sad demeanour, to the chantry.
Before he leaves the holy place,
The servant has run off apace
To tell her all his observations –
The mourning, grief and lamentations
That Eliduc made there, alone.

The lady, almost overthrown,
Says
        "We will go at once to search,

243

Both inside and outside the church.
My lord will soon be on his way
He must talk with the King today.
The hermit died a while ago.
My husband loved him well, I know –
Yet something more, it's my belief,
Has caused him this excessive grief."

The King needs to consult him soon
He rides to court that afternoon.
She goes to find his place of prayer
Her serving man directs her there.
Into the oratory they pass,
And there she sees the lovely lass
Still on her bed, in death-like pose,
Her face a newly opened rose.

She lifts the cloak that is her pall
Sees her young figure, lissom, small,
Arms and hands, long, white and slender
Tapered fingers, slim and tender.
Seeing at once the truth behind
Her husband's wretchedness of mind,
She calls the servant in to witness
The wondrous cause of his distress.

"Look! Do you see this pretty girl
As flawless as a precious pearl?
To look upon her is great pleasure.
She was my husband's joy and treasure,
For her sweet sake, he mourned and pined;
It's no great wonder, to my mind,
When such a lovely woman dies.
The tears well up in my own eyes –
For pity or sorrow, I can't say.
This sight takes all my joy away
Never to see a happy day."
By the bier-side, reverent,
She bows in sorrow, to lament
A life so fair and transient.

As she stays praying on her knees,
Before her eyes, scurries a weasel
From underneath the altar frontal.
It runs across the maiden's bed
And with its feet defiles the dead.

– Vicious, dirty little vermin
Unlike the pure and snow-white ermine –
At least, the footman thinks it so,
And with his stick he strikes one blow
Which knocks it dead. He flings the wretch
Across the floor.

      This seems to fetch
A second weasel from its hole. Her
Mate's plight causes her great dolour.
She runs to his carcass, weaving round it,
Tries ineffectually to rouse it –
Dabbing and prodding with her paw,
She pats its head. But there's no more
That she can do to bring relief.
He lies stone dead. In seeming grief
She scuttles off among the trees
In search of magic remedies.

Among the herbs, one in a million,
She finds a flower of deep vermilion.
Snipping the stem with her sharp bite
She rushes back, fast as she might,
To the corpse of her slaughtered mate
The victim of a cruel fate.
She puts the red flower in his jaws –
How rapidly this herb restores!

Guildelüec, in her astonishment
Quick as a flash calls an admonishment:
"Stop them! Oh, catch them if you can
Don't let them get away, young man!"
The servant makes one desperate throw
Striking the male a glancing blow.
He lets the precious blossom fall
They scamper off, once and for all.

The lady, leaving the death bed,
Collects the herb – so ruby red,
So beautiful, and with such power.
She places the enchanted flower
On the girl's lips. A short suspense
Is broken.
　　　　　　She regains her senses,
Stirs, breathes, moans. Opens her eyes.
"God, I have slept so long!" she cries.
Guildelüec, when she hears this phrase,
Offers to God her thanks and praise
And asks the girl who she might be.

"I was born in Logres, lady,
The King's child; and I loved the knight
Sir Eliduc, a man of might
In the paid service of the court.
It was my love for him that brought
Me here. But he had lied to me
I thought I was his bride-to-be.
He, who was already wed!

"I never dreamed; he never said
Or gave a sign he had a wife.
When, for the first time in my life
I heard of it, in my great grief,
I swooned, collapsed. Alas, how base
To leave me in this dismal place,
Abandoned, quite alone and friendless,
The traitor's villainy is endless!
I can't but think that men are cruel,
And she who trusts them is a fool."

"Sweet child," Guildelüec replies
"This is the truth, I speak no lies;
Eliduc's cast down with grief,
Nothing on earth can bring relief.
For certain, it's his firm belief
That you are dead. Each day, my dear,
Weeping, he came to see you here

247

When you lay cold, bereft of life.
Believe me –
      for I am his wife.

"My heart broke for him in his woe.
Day after day, he'd leave and go,
Till I resolved that I must know
What dreadful thing had grieved him so.
I followed him, and here – found you.
I rejoice that you're restored;
Now, come with me to greet that lord
Who once was mine, and now is yours.
He'll have the Princess he adores.
I will dissolve our marriage troth
For the happiness of you both.
A love like yours is no betrayal.

"I am resolved to take the veil;
Nothing could better please me now
That to make Christ my solemn vow,
For it has long been in my mind
To leave all worldly ties behind."
With every comfort she can say
She calms her, till they take their way.

The squire is sent off, to report
To Eliduc at the Breton court.
Greeting him, he tells his lord
The Princess' life is quite restored.
At this bewildering discourse
Our hero sends for a fresh horse.
Without an escort guard, the knight
Rides off at once.

              He's home by night;
In loving-kindness, thanks his wife.
To see the girl restored to life
Brings joy too wondrous to express.
He's never known such happiness.
He can't stop kissing the Princess

And she responds with tenderness.
Their reunion is blissful.

Guildelüec is sweetly wistful.
She knows, now, that the time is right
To make agreement with the knight.
She asks for freedom to depart
Follow the calling of her heart
To be a nun, and serve the Lord.
She hopes they'll come to an accord –
If he will grant her land, she'll raise
A monastery in God's praise
And there, in peace, she'll pass her days.

Then Eliduc may freely wed
His love. For it's a sin, she said,
To take two spouses to one's bed
And to maintain a double life;
By law, a man has but one wife.
Our hero heartily agrees
To grant Guildelüec release.
He gladly gives, with open hand,
A very handsome piece of land
Near his château, in the wood
Where the hermit's chapel stood.

Here, in this large and pleasant space
Where such a miracle took place,
The monastery church is founded
Houses and cloisters set around it;
Endowed with wealth and title deeds
To land and everything it needs.
When the building work is done
She dons the habit of a nun;
With thirty sisters, takes her vows,
Establishes her convent house,
Plans their religious discipline
For simple, chaste, industrious living.

This noble lai is almost done.

Eliduc weds Guilliadun:
With dignity they solemnise
Their marriage vows before all eyes.
More feasts and pomp than I can say
Crown this most joyous wedding day.
In perfect love, so it appears,
They lived for many happy years;
In charity, at their expense,
Dispensing great munificence.
Until at last they reached an age
To think of their last pilgrimage.

They turned their minds to heaven above
And to the service of God's love.
After much thought, the good knight planned
A second minster on his land
Built on the castle's other side
With everything he could provide.
He endowed most of his estate
And all his gold and silver plate.
His own retainers, with some more
Devout kind souls become the core
To keep the rule of this community
In godly worship, peace and unity.

When everything is well-prepared
Without delay, the noble lord
With his good brethren vows his soul
Evermore to serve the holy
Merciful and one true God.
He pledges heart and mind and body.
As he accepts monastic life
The Reverend Mother, his first wife,
Agrees that Lady Guilliadun
May join her as a sister nun.
Mother Guildelüec warmly greets her
In God's service she will teach her;
She's received by the sorority
With honour, tenderness and amity.

They pray together for God's grace
On the dear founder of this place;
The knight prays likewise for their souls
Thus God grants mercy, and consoles.
A messenger is often sent
For news of how their two lives went
And of their spiritual well-being.

Each strove to serve the great all-seeing
With truth, fidelity and love.
When they at last were called above
In peace they drew their final breath
In hope and charity and faith.
Thanks be to God, for such a death.

So ends the history of these three.
The courtly bard of Brittany
Composed this most affecting lai
– Of its kind, a nonpareil–
That those who hear or read this song
May remember well, and long.
God send you all a loving friend,
And, in ripe time, a happy end.

FINIS

COMMENTARY

These essays are observations, not scholarly notes. My personal impressions are, in the main, completely unverifiable. Nevertheless, they work for me, and this book is written in the light of these insights. I've tried to establish a mode and tone for each lai. You are entitled to know the thought-processes that went into them.

Most of the lais have literary parallels, but few have surviving antecedents. Academic research requires concrete evidence; documents, maps, stylistic chronology, linguistic clues. I'm not in a position to provide these.

Ideas and images are like visitations; not always the kind of thing you can describe in a thesis. Verse translation is done with ear and voice, relying as much upon informed instinct and intuition as it does upon literal meaning. Ultimately, what matters is the poetry.

Within every work of art are clues to its origins. Stories grow, and part of the content of each tale reaches back to its original teller. When working on *Yonec*, I stood on a hill and saw the silver city in a modern industrial landscape. I can't prove where and why the werewolf Bisclavret hides his clothes under a big stone. But deep down, I know the answer.

PROLOGUE TO THE LAIS

I kept deferring the task of translating Marie's Prologue, which has some notoriously obscure passages. Even worse, taken at face value, the Prologue is humourless, grim and sententious. Who nowadays knows or cares about Priscian's Latin grammar? How to lose readers – begin your book of magical love-stories with a scholarly sermon!

Looking for my way in, I read the Prologue over and over, comparing the Old French with various English translations. It seemed to me that the only way to engage the modern reader would be to write a parody. After it was finished, I learned that mediaeval prologues were often spoofs. The writer would drone on about the moral value of the work, and the toil and anguish of writing it, thus laying claim to high seriousness.

I've made additions and jokes of my own, all of which should be detectable to the alert reader. For example, Marie really does say :

> If someone wants to avoid vice, he should work hard at his studies
> and take on a challenging project. Thus he can divert himself from
> paths which lead to personal anguish. That's why I began thinking
> about writing some worthy story from Latin into French.

Vice? Marie de France? If you take the starched-wimple view of mediaeval women, it's like imagining Jane Austen taking opium and romping in bed with Lord Byron. It seemed natural to bring in the typical mediaeval motif of the Seven Deadly Sins.

Yet Marie invokes her own experience here, so I began to consider the vices that afflict artists. The obvious one was accidie, a melancholic lassitude. In other words, writer's block, the very reason that started me writing translations as an exercise.

In plain modern English, Marie's opening lines are bossy:

> A person who has been given knowledge and good communication
> skills ought not to keep silent and aloof, but should gladly
> demonstrate these abilities.

But in Marie's own voice, they are a clarion call: - Don't fritter your talents away.

> *Ki Deus ad duné escïence*
> *E de parler bon'eloquence*
> *Ne s'en deit taisir ne celer,*
> *Ainz se deit volunters mustrer.*

Whoever has a poet's voice
And, by the grace of God, enjoys
The gift of learning, holds in trust
A precious treasure, which she must
Not hide away, lest moths and rust
Corrupt it and it turns to dust.

I : GUIGEMAR

Marie's collection of *Lais* begins and ends with poems of novella length. *Guigemar* is about youthful discovery, *Eliduc* is a tale of redemptive maturity. Spring and autumn. We begin the book by riding out of a castle, and end by walking into an abbey.

Most people look on first love, agony and all, with glowing nostalgia. This is the tone of my version of *Guigemar*, which I see in the light and colour of a clear bright morning. The hero's quest for healing resembles episodes from the Tristan stories, without the sense of tragic inevitability. Adulthood lived in despair is perpetual torment. The follies and sharp pangs of youth pass, and we learn from them. Guigemar travels with a blind trust in fortune. Tristan and Iseult are cunning and must plan ahead simply to survive. The lad Guigemar is the antithesis of the man Tristan's trickster persona.

There are two magic elements in this story, the stricken white deer and the marvellous ship. Both are manifestations of fortune. The hind's dying curse conceals a blessing. Marie's words give a lilt to this passage; literal translation would erase its solemnity. I've made it a spell of enchantment:

> ... *Oï, lase! jo sui ocise!*
> *E tu, vassal, ki m'as nafree,*
> *Tel seit la tue destinee:*
> *Jamais n'aies tu med[e]cine!*
> *Ne par herbe ne par racine*
> *Ne par mire ne par pociun*
> *N'avras tu jamés garisun ...*

> ... Alas! I'm wounded near to death
> The victim of Man's cruelty.
> And you, the wretch who murdered me
> I shall foretell your destiny:–
> Your wound shall have no remedy
> Your pain and anguish none can calm
> No healing herb, no magic charm
> Nor leaf, nor root, nor soothing balm
> No doctor can allay your harm ...

To point up Marie's theme of fortune, I name the magic boat the Silver Hind, an anachronism recalling Sir Francis Drake's galleon, the Golden Hind. In the Greek myth, one of the labours of Herakles was to capture alive the bronze-hoofed Ceryneian Hind, which bore on its head the golden antlers of a male deer. After a year's chase, Herakles wounds her with an arrow. Since the creature is sacred to Artemis, this gets Herakles in trouble with the goddess. He appeases her by releasing the hind in such a way that he fulfils the terms of his challenge, while allowing the deer to run back to her mistress.

Marie de France knew her classics, but *Guigemar* need not be a direct reference to the Greek story. The hunt of pure white fairy animals haunts Celtic tales. Yet the similarities with Herakles speak to me of the deep-downness of story in the human psyche. The link here is hunting. Our hunter-gatherer ancestors killed animals for food; in some cultures they enacted rites to thank or appease the dead animal's spirit, in order to ensure further kills. Hierarchical urban societies turned hunting into a costly aristocratic sport with elaborate insider rituals, and cruel punishments for poaching.

Guigemar hunts for the thrill of the chase; his ostensible quarry is venison for the pot. When he kills the hind, he is leaving the fawn to starve; such wastefulness breaks an ancient taboo. The quest turns out to be his rite of passage. Our sports-mad teenage virgin hero is indifferent to emotion.   Through hardship, he will at last find his first, passionate and enduring love.

The dawning of young love might be considered a struggle between Artemis (Diana), goddess of hunting and chastity, and Aphrodite (Venus), goddess of love. In *Guigemar* the miserly husband has his wife's room painted with images of Venus burning Ovid's ironic self-help manual for the heartbroken, *Love's Remedy*. Venus punishes those who flout her power. The wife's generous interpretation of this message is the opposite of her husband's intention. Once he's crossed love's threshold, Guigemar becomes and remains a loyal servant of the goddess.

Marie simply states that fortune's ship sails from Brittany into the unknown. Cornwall has strong ancient links with Brittany.   The nearest magical destination would be the fabled land of Lyonesse, not far from where we live and work.   (See Apsley's drawing).

Guigemar and his lady exchange tokens which apparently have magic powers. Her locked girdle and his knotted shirt will ensure fidelity when the two are forced to part. I've added lovers' banter to their dialogue, to emphasise their complete trust in one another. These gifts are literary symbols of their loving constancy. It strikes me as odd that, while the lady must wear her magic girdle all the time, Guigemar has to send his manservant to fetch the shirt when the time comes for his true-love to untie the knot.

Don't even think of calling the lady's girdle a chastity belt. Marie de France's enchanting story has nothing to do with that vile contraption, which has been proved to be a myth. The popular image of the knightly crusader going off to war, leaving his wife confined in steel bands, is a nonsense. Crusaders committed appalling atrocities, but not, it seems, this piece of cruelty to women.

There are no genuine mediaeval chastity belts, nor is there documentary evidence. I've read that one or two Italian Renaissance specimens exist. It's thought that women possessed them for use only in situations of extreme danger. The victors of a siege would have no scruples about wholesale rape.

II : EQUITAN

General opinion is that *Equitan* derives from the tradition of the *fabliau*, a comic story (usually coarse) in verse.   The most hilarious example is Chaucer's *Miller's Tale*.

In Marie's version of the story, king Equitan and the seneschal's wife start out as two ordinary, well-liked courtly people. Equitan's favourite pastimes are hunting and dalliance. Because he enjoys the pleasures of love, he remains true to the code of chivalry. For he knows that :

Cil met[ent] lur vie en nu[n]cure

Que d'amur n'unt sen e mesure;
Tels est la mesure de amer
Que nul n'i deit reisun garder.

Stupid folk love recklessly
And put their lives in jeopardy;
Love's ardent power is so great
That reason bends beneath its weight

It's only after he falls immoderately in love with Mme. Seneschal that he falls into temptation and loses his mind. This mediaeval morality tale could be the plot of a film noir like *Double Indemnity*. But it doesn't quite work for me. It's just so much funnier if Equitan is a cad and a rotter from the start, and rogers his heartless way through life until his uppance is finally come.

Marie tells this story absolutely straight, making it hard for many readers to take. After repeated readings, I still hated it. A cheating couple plot murder by the most diabolical means, and fall into their own trap. They're scalded to death. Serve them right. That's what you get if you try to bump someone off. Marie ends with a brisk done-and-dusted flourish, like an old-fashioned nurse tucking in bed-sheets:

Ki bien vodreit reisun entendre,
Ici purreit ensample prendre:
Tel purcace le mal d'autrui
Dunt le mals [tut] revert sur lui.

The wise will take example from this moral :- He who plots harm against another may find his wickedness returns to haunt him.

How could I avoid a nasty sermonizing tone? Or make agonized death a satisfying ending? Torture and cruelty aren't funny. I decided the only way *Equitan* would work for me would be to rewrite it in the *fabliau* style, keeping to the story, but turning it into bedroom farce. Hooray for the jolly British tradition of smutty seaside postcards and the *Carry On* films.

Despite this re-working, I've stayed close to the tone and wording of key passages in the original. These are the scenes in which the couple expose their venal, self-serving attitudes to love. In the lais, Marie often employs reported speech; more dramatic utterance is kept for moments of decision, revelation or tension. Marie uses direct speech for Equitan's sleepless night monologue, and dialogue for his debate with the lady. Their conversation gives witty insights into their self-justifying folie à deux.

My version keeps the essentials of these set-pieces; I just embroider them for comic effect. Audiences in Marie de France's day would quickly spot the ironies in this story. At first we're told that Equitan and the lady possess the usual virtues; in their behaviour they transgress them all. Nowadays readers might well miss these subtle indications.

Marie says she heard the lais performed by Breton jongleurs. Storytellers improvise; if a joke or a theme is going down well with the audience, a performer elaborates on it, makes a running gag or a refrain out of it. I've turned the climax of *Equitan* into a fugue of pantomime puns.

There may be hidden clues to the jongleur's humour in the text. Equitan's name suggests an equestrian, a horseman with all the sexual connotations of the word "ride". I could have

255

called him Easy Rider.

Equitan's kingdom is Nauns, usually translated as the region around Nantes. One study suggests it may be a corruption of *nains*, making him the king of dwarves. I don't follow the dwarf theory in this translation of the poem, but it has interesting possibilities. Shakespeare's characterisation of Richard III depends on the superstition that that bodily appearance mirrored the state of the soul. The sexually maimed Fisher King rules over the Waste Land. Dwarves in mediaeval poems are usually treacherous, just as lepers are lascivious. Equitan is a moral pigmy; his randiness might be compensation for a size problem. I'm not making fun of people with growth disorders. Napoleon and Hitler were short men. Equitan was a beastly little runt. Another rhyming opportunity missed.

III : LE FRESNE

Most of Marie's significant male characters are named. But she gives proper names to only three of her leading women; the others are just the lady, the maiden, the wife, the princess. Le Fresne is Marie's most affecting heroine, but even her name is no more than a soubriquet; the baby girl is called after the tree where she's found.

To call her Le Fresne throughout sounds clumsy to the English ear, but then, so does Ash-Tree. It felt important to keep the fairy-tale strangeness of the name, but I wanted to give it a pleasingly feminine sound. Ashley was suggested, but it's a name for both sexes. The story is in the Cinderella tradition. It's a nice coincidence that in English, Ash means both tree and cinders. In German, Cinderella is Aschenputtel, and in Scots, Assipattle. In the end, I chose the name Ashling.

To suit the folk-tale atmosphere, I've made changes in location and characterisation. The original story is set at Dol de Bretagne in north-east Brittany, not far from Mont St. Michel. I've never been to this beautiful mediaeval town. Yet I wanted a familiar landscape setting for *Le Fresne*, especially for the nursemaid's journey. One of the more plausible identifications of Marie de France is that she might have been Marie, Abbess of Shaftesbury. Since I grew up in North Dorset, just a few miles away, I played "What if?"

Like Dol, Shaftesbury is a handsome ancient town. Some Wessex people still use the alternative name, Shaston, as does Thomas Hardy in *Tess of the D'Urbervilles*. The town stands on a high, steep hill overlooking Blackmore Vale, the flood-plain of the river Stour. This almost impregnable site was a Saxon stronghold. In 888AD, King Alfred founded the Benedictine nunnery. His daughter Aethelgeofu was the first abbess of Shaftesbury.

The abbey ruins have a magnificent view from the sandstone escarpment, in places almost a precipice, which rises out of the pastures of Blackmore Vale. The river Stour floods every winter. In the centuries before agricultural drainage, the land surrounding Shaftesbury Hill would have been treacherously boggy. Under the hill, the road across Shaftesbury Common is raised up like a causeway.

Journeys come alive when the landscape is described. Marie simply says the nurse carries the baby along a broad track through the woods until she reaches a town with an abbey. Unless it's an old Roman road, the path's going to be a muddy, rutted, filthy mess, with roots and stones to trip her up, and thorns to snag her clothes. No paved roads, no lights, thick woods seething with wild beasts. This is the superstitious 12th century – there'd be spooks, man-traps, outlaws, witches, gibbeted felons. No wonder the nanny is delighted to hear sounds of civilisation:

Bien loinz sur destre aveit oï
Chiens abaier e coks chanter:
Iloc purrat vile trover.

Far on the hill, as day is dawning,
Cocks start to crow to greet the morning.
Hounds bay, dogs give a cheerful bark
That seems to drive away the dark.
The nurse is much relieved to hear
These sounds come from a township near.

That brief description is one of my favourite passages in Marie de France. Most of her sensory observations are of courtly settings, or glimpses into the fabulous Otherworld. She spends a lot of time describing sumptuous objects and telling us how much they are worth. From this homely glimpse of everyday life, I draw my folk-tale tone.

In mediaeval stories, incidental characters are usually little more than plot devices; they walk on, play their small part in the narrative, and disappear. Once they've delivered the message or imparted good advice, the reader gives these figures no more thought. In *Le Fresne*, there are two such characters, on whom the progress of the story depends. I felt they needed to satisfy some archetype or persona embedded in our cultural unconscious, as the characters in fairy-tales do.

The first of these bit-part actors is the maid who rescues the infant Ashling. We're told she comes from a noble family. The text is ambiguous. The woman could be a young maidservant, a favoured protegée of the lady. Or she could be the lady's old nanny, now about to take charge of the next generation. I find the latter explanation much more satisfying and interesting.

To me, the maidservant is an earthy fairy godmother; middle-aged, plump, bustling, sweet-natured, full of no-nonsense advice. She has cared for the lady since infancy, and the bond is strong. Naturally she'd use baby-talk, whether cooing to the new-born twins or calming their hysterical mother.

She shows heroic devotion to the lady. It's dangerous enough for the nanny to smuggle a tiny baby out of a castle. Then she has to traipse miles through the forest by night. What if she's walking to Shaftesbury? After her muddy trek, she has to climb a steep cobbled hill. Why, Gold Hill, of course, made famous in the Hovis bread advertisement.

You'll have noticed that I've given the abbey porter a Dorset accent, as authentic as memory and the great 19th century dialect poet William Barnes can make it. It's the warm, buttery voice of people I knew as a child. This good fellow is surely not a Norman gentleman in holy orders – he lives humbly at home with his daughter and grandson. No, he's a honest, trustworthy local man employed by the nunnery. Jokingly, I think of him as one of the earliest working-class characters in literature. He plays such an important, caring role in the story that he deserves a more fully-rounded portrayal.

Le Fresne is sometimes likened to *Patient Griselda*, a character in later mediaeval poems, Boccaccio's *Decameron* and Chaucer's *Clerk's Tale*. *Patient Griselda* is a morality tale which I, like a sensible woman, hate. Griselda, a beautiful commoner, is married to an aristocrat who tests her virtue to a cruel degree. He hides away their children, telling Griselda that they're dead. He fakes a second marriage and orders Griselda to wait on his new bride. Then he reveals all: the bride is their own daughter. Griselda's patience under these trials has proved her a worthy and obedient wife. And he takes her back, and she loves him still and they live happily ever after. As if. Fortunately the grim story is leavened by Chaucer's irony.

257

The similarities in these stories are only skin-deep. Gurun doesn't set tests or play callous mind-games with Le Fresne. *Lai Le Fresne* belongs to the world-wide host of Cinderellas: a girl of wise and benevolent character is reunited with her love.

Gurun's not a obsessive tyrant. His behaviour to Le Fresne, at first decisive and manly, turns weak and irresolute. The couple are so far childless, so Gurun decides he must seek a wife to bear him heirs. He's encouraged in this plan by the knights in his retinue. They have good cause; if Gurun dies without successors, his estates will pass to another lord. An in-comer would bring his own entourage, displacing Gurun's men. In this dilemma, Gurun gives his duty to his team precedence over loyalty to his lover. It's a man thing.

Le Fresne is not a resourceful girl in the active sense, but she has sterling qualities: tact, wisdom, compassion, character and charm. Gurun's followers love her, so I imagine her to be a cheerful person with a considerate nature. Perhaps she enjoys the occasional bit of backchat with this band of soldiers.

Her real strength is her integrity. Being a foundling, it must have been hard to establish her sense of self. At the turning point of the story, she still has no idea of her parentage or origin. Through her aunt's teaching, Le Fresne has learned fortitude; she's able to mask her emotions and get on with life. The well-being of her lover is her paramount concern, and with superhuman restraint, she conceals her own heartbreak. Nothing must be allowed to interfere with the preparations for his wedding day.

Le Fresne's wise forbearance is born of experience and love. By contrast, patience is one the dreariest of the seven deadly virtues, on a par with chastity and obedience. Gurun is blessed in his wife. It's a good match, and we just know that their marriage will grow closer and stronger. Patient Griselda's husband will surely remain an unredeemed paranoid bully.

IV : BISCLAVRET

As I began writing this essay, BBC radio announced that a wolf had escaped from a wild-life park in Devon: "This animal is not dangerous unless cornered. Nevertheless, the public should be on the alert."

I love *Bisclavret*, but when young I resisted its magic. Perhaps the flowery Edwardian translation, the only one available at that time, had something to do with it. I like my werewolves full-on. It seems to me that the shape-shifter's tragedy lies not in his exile from humanity, but in the sunrise summons to relinquish wildness and return to the humdrum.

Ideas of narrative have changed over time. In the mediaeval period, there was no such concept as psychology. When creating personae, early writers gave little thought to individual traits and interior motivation. Leading characters were composites of a set of conventional virtues and their corresponding vices. It's only by repeated readings, in the Old French and in various translations, that I've come to realise that Marie de France is a shrewd observer of human nature. Fantasy though it is, *Bisclavret* rings true. It's possible that Marie is creating satirical characters based on people she actually knew.

There's something all too recognisable about this mismatched couple. Bisclavret feels trapped by the commitment of marriage; his wife feigns that helpless infantilism which too often passes for femininity. He is brooding, introspective and independent, she is clinging and emotionally manipulative.

My version recalls modern depictions of such couples. One of P G Wodehouse's funniest creations is the appalling Madeline Basset, with her wheedling manner and affected lisp. She believes in fairies and deludes herself that poor Bertie Wooster is in love with her. I've introduced Madeline's reproachful "Oh, how could you..." tone into the dialogue.

As a student first reading *Bisclavret*, it seemed to me as if Bisclavret had sold out his ancient heritage. The dark beast belongs in the land of Long Ago, and his presence in the courtly world emasculates him.   In the heady days of the late 1960's, I felt Marie de France was preaching at me, exploiting an archaic legend for conservative moral ends.

But this is to take Marie's lai too solemnly. Her werewolf is an emblem, not an ancestral archetype. Through the medium of the old story, Marie explores the nature of love and trust, while playfully reversing our expectations at every turn. Throughout, we ask ourselves : Who's the villain, who's the victim? Where do our sympathies lie? Readers must find their own answer. There's no heavy-handed moralising here.

Yet, much as I now enjoy the subtle wit and sophistication of Marie's interpretation, the underlying fantasy still fascinates me. Shape-shifters are found in every culture. Their images appear in early cave paintings. Perhaps they are a folk-memory of shamans, seers, priests and healers; men and women who embody the knowledge and lore of their people. They know and use the means to communicate with, and enter into, the otherworld and the realm of the ancestors.

Although Marie gives no location for *Bisclavret*, I believe that this tale must once have been connected with a particular place. The Wolf's lair is in the precincts of a old chapel. He hides his clothes nearby, in a broad hollow stone concealed by bushes. This stone is a threshold through which he passes between worlds. Marie's brief description contains enough detail to indicate a prehistoric site which had been Christianized at a much later date. It's not unusual to find churches built on ancient ritual landscapes, burial mounds and pagan holy wells.

The Wolf's hiding place calls to mind a distinct type of megalithic structure. A dolmen is a chamber created by setting a number of large stones upright to carry a massive slab. Dolmens are Neolithic or early Bronze Age in date; very roughly from 4,000-2,500 BC. This period is long before any cultural evidence which could be described as Celtic. Dolmens are usually said to be funerary monuments, but no-one really knows their purpose, or the beliefs of the people who built them. Most likely the stones honoured the ancestors whose spirits dwelt in that place, keeping watch over the living. Every generation since their making must have made legends about these marvellous edifices.

In the Breton language: *Dol Men* = table-stone. In Cornish *Tol Men* = hole-y stone or hollow stone.   Maybe the twin Celtic languages, Cornish and Breton, hold a lost pun, since table and hollow both describe a dolmen perfectly. Apsley's illustration places Bisclavret beside Lanyon Quoit in West Cornwall, though the Wolf may just as well have stood by a dolmen in Brittany. These monuments dot the landscape of western Europe, with concentrations in Wales, Brittany, Ireland and Cornwall.

> *Une vielz chapele i esteit,*
> *Ke meintefeiz grant bien me feit:*
> *La est la piere cruose e lee*
> *Suz un buissun, dedenz cavee …*

An old chapel is there, which has often stood me in good stead.
There is a hollow, broad stone, under a bush, recessed inside …

Why does Bisclavret choose this place? The clue lies in the second line. Bisclavret's den is of practical use to him, but it also gives him spiritual comfort in his unhallowed bestial state. He leaves his human clothing under the protection of the Christian trinity and of Mary mother of Jesus. But he's also invoking the ancestral guardians of place, the old spirits, gods and goddesses.

Early Christian settlements were sometimes placed in association with prehistoric features like barrow-mounds, healing springs, earthworks and standing stones. Celtic Christians became part of a continuous tradition of reverence and worship. Sacred wells carried on their healing work; only the name of their tutelary god was changed.

The poem begins with a spine-chilling passage, describing the habits of werewolves, and assuring us that they once were plentiful and are still roaming at large. It's Marie's "Hungarian sneeze", the teller's device to make us suspend our disbelief. After that teasing build-up, Marie tells the tale in her spare, matter-of-fact style. Even when his wife talks Bisclavret into revealing his secret, the dialogue is unsensational. You'd expect Madame B to be climbing the walls crazed with fear, but no, she stays calm and just keeps on pressing him for more details.

I ask myself this question – Would the jongleurs have performed *Bisclavret* deadpan?

To which the answer flies back – Not bloody likely!

Consider the end of the poem. We learn that the villainous pair were banished to a distant country. There they bred a large family of children, who visibly took after their parents. Marie simply writes:

> (Many of the female line)
> It's true, were born without noses
> And went through life noseless.

Now look at the original couplet. I challenge you to read these lines aloud to your friends, without giggling, while holding your nose. (Of course it works best in a flawless 12th century Anglo-Norman accent, like mine.)   It goes like this:-

> ...*C'est verité, senz nes sunt nees*
> *E si viveient esnasees.*

Can it be accidental that Marie chose such absurdly nasal words? This couplet is a clue to her sense of fun. I'm convinced that in this comic phrasing she is recollecting and imitating a trick of the jongleurs' trade. It's intended as a hint to storytellers and readers-aloud. And it still works!

When I first spotted the joke, I hoped that Marie had coined the strange word *esnasee* (dis-nosed). But the *Larousse Dictionnaire de l'Ancien Français* cites the verb *esnaser* in another, earlier, context. Mutilation was a common punishment, so perhaps the word was, horribly, in regular usage.

Chases and scenes of brouhaha are a gift, allowing the storyteller to include running gags, flights of invention and improvisation. When the Sage gives the King wise advice, I picture the rhetoric and suspense of a TV courtroom drama, culminating as the Sage turns and points dramatically to denounce the wicked wife.

Imagine All Hallows Eve, Hallowe'en, the Celtic Samhain. As the year turns to winter, families and communities remember their dead.   After the evening meal, a grizzled grandad is playing at being fierce, growling and chasing the children round the table.   He's wearing a wolf-skin cloak, boasting to his eldest grandson "He was my first wolf. I shot him when I was just about your age." He tells them a story. When he gets to the bit where the wolf bites the lady, he plays an old trick on the little ones; he pinches their faces and with his thumb folded in his fist, he brandishes their bitten-off noses. Squeals of play-fear and delight.

What about the escaped wolf in Devon? Within hours he was successfully recaptured, unharmed, by marksmen with tranquilliser darts. One charming detail : the wolf's name is Parker. His nom de plume, says Apsley.

V : LANVAL

Lanval has the most satisfying ending of any story I know. It's the archetypal Breton lai, a romance of love and adventure at the intersection between worlds.

Guigemar is a quest and *Lanval* is a romance; they are both stories about youth and first love. Young Guigemar is impulsive, Lanval is introspective. Guigemar's pain comes from a thigh wound which he brings on himself by shooting the fairy deer. A gracious woman heals Guigemar and initiates him in love.

In contrast, Lanval's misery is visited upon him by the negligent treatment he receives at Arthur's court. Lanval's rite of passage is poised between fantasy and reality. The golden age is over; chivalry has grown shabby, vitiated. His dreams of glory at the Round Table are shattered. He can find no place or purpose for himself in this world. At the nadir of despair, he encounters the Otherworld Lady. In his disillusionment, the young knight meets an illusion.

She's a fairy, of course, though because of its tinsel associations, I use that word only once. Since the language should convey the magic of this fairytale romance, I've allowed myself more archaisms in this poem than in any of the others. When I began translating the *Lais*, I swore never to use words like *damsel*, *swain* and *varlet*. If you find them in the finished work, assume they are ironic – except in *Lanval*. *Damsel* occurs nine times in this book, eight of which are in *Lanval*. The damsels are all fairies of unearthly beauty and grace.

Marie doesn't tell us directly through words and symbols, that Lanval's lady is from Elfland. In a Scottish ballad like *Thomas the Rhymer*, the fairy would be dressed all in green, and her horse would be decked with silver bells. In Celtic folk-lore, green is the fairy colour of choice, though I don't know if *vert* has the same significance in French. The Lady's skin is as white as hawthorn blossom, and she uses a fur cloak to shield herself from the sun. A pale complexion is the mark of a noblewoman, who does no hard outdoor work to burn the skin and roughen the hands. Or perhaps the Lady can't face the sun because she comes from the fairy realm under earth, where the light is supernatural.

She is reclining in an impossibly extravagant tent, and drapes herself in rich fur and exotic silk. Marie de France lavishes detail on descriptions of wealth, in both magical and Christian contexts – fairy ship, grand abbey. An obsession with treasure strikes me as a typical early mediaeval theme. Any fighting men in the audience would have pricked up their ears at the mention of loot. Elfland is a place of fabulous riches, which fairies sometimes lend to humans, as long as they keep to the conditions set.

The Otherworld Lady is characterised by her abandonment of conventional modesty. She casts the fairy aura of glamour. Yet we see at once, just as Lanval does, that her beauty is truth. Her cloak of white ermine fur is a symbol of purity. There's no coyness or debate. The two lovers offer themselves up to one another with candour and complete naturalness. They are destined to be together, and this is their time and place.

Fairy gifts have strings attached. Lanval's pledge not to speak of his love is a sacred taboo (*geis* in Irish). His punishment for failing to comply is to lose everything, even the will to live. But his Lady is merciful enough to forgive him. She exonerates Lanval and humiliates Arthur's Queen by baring herself in front of the assembled court. In this act there is no shamelessness, for shame is quite irrelevant. The Lady is a nature spirit, and her beauty is something to be held in reverence.

There's only one significant Christian reference in this poem. Ironically it comes at the moment when the Queen rages at Lanval:

Mut est mi sires maubailliz
Que pres de lui vus ad suffert;
Mun escïent que Deus en pert!

King Arthur's spotless reputation
Is tarnished by association.
I even fear for his salvation!

This is hypocrisy of the nastiest kind. First the Queen slanders Lanval with a false attempt to "out" him. Then she invokes God to support her lies. She's trapped in her wounded pride. Her falsehood grows out of control until she believes her own histrionics.

Even the most decent, liberal young man is likely to be hurt by gibes about his sexuality. And men who have been rebuffed by women still resort to the "you're frigid" or "she's a lesbian" level of debate. The Queen has the same angry reflex. This kind of insult is, apparently, a recognised motif in mediaeval narratives. Marie uses explicit wording for the Queen's spiteful allegations :

Vallez avez bien afeitiez,
Ensemble od eus vus deduiez.

You slake your infamous desires
With pretty serving boys and squires.

No-one should imagine Marie de France as an unworldly person. She lived in robust times. Even so, I imagine that this scene might have shocked her audience and readers to the core. I wonder – should a mediaeval lady even have known about gay sex, let alone publicly written of it? It's like Mary Crawford's "rears and vices" joke about the navy, in *Mansfield Park*. Did Jane Austen, of all people, write that?

There have been times in the history of European Christendom when publicly to label a man a homosexual was tantamount to a death sentence. The Queen surely knew what she was doing. In the 12th century, the church was perhaps less intolerant than it later became. Marriage was about begetting heirs, not love. Many knights and crusaders must have found true solace in the arms of their companions. But I don't believe the church would have officially condoned this. It's still debating the subject today.

Nowadays, how does one now convey the frisson of the Queen's slander? One can no more "accuse" a person of being gay than one can accuse them of having curly hair or being Icelandic. I've chosen to use the ugly language of homophobia. It shocks – and we know whose side we're on.

Lanval was popular. There are extant translations in Middle English and Old Norse. The best known English version is *Sir Launfal*, by Thomas Chestre, which dates from the late 14th century. In *Sir Launfal*, there's more jousting, less love. In its field, it's well-known, but to my ear, the poetry isn't a patch on Marie's glittering work. Thomas Chestre's Queen just spits out a random string of insults, but Marie's Guinevere thinks it through. Her words strike straight to the heart.

"Lanval" fet ele, "Bien le quit,
Vuz n'amez gueres cel delit;

Asiz le m'ad hum dit sovent
Que des femmez n'avez talent.
Vallez avez bien afeitiez,
Ensemble od eus vus deduiez.
Vileins cuarz, mauveis failliz,
Mut est mi sires maubailliz
Que pres de lui vus ad suffert;
Mun escïent que Deus en pert!"

"I know your sort!
It's common gossip in the court
You've other outlets for your sport.
Of course you've never fancied women –
You've got a bunch of hand-picked yeomen!
You slake your infamous desires
With pretty serving boys and squires.
Why did you ever turn up here
You snivelling, skulking, craven queer!
King Arthur's spotless reputation
Is tarnished by association.
I even fear for his salvation!
God sees the company he keeps
With such a sinful little creep."

VI : LES DEUS AMANZ

He is *sages, pruz e beus*, she is *pruz e sage e bele*. Bless them, such wisdom, beauty, charm and resourcefulness in two such sweet young things. They're still going through the torments of adolescence. She's worried about her weight, he's anxious about his weedy frame. At last they find each other, a friend who understands. We've all been there.

Deus Amanz follows Marie's theme of love in *mesure* and *démesure*, moderation and excess. The widowed King's only comfort is his daughter. As in many fairy-tales, his love for her has incestuous undertones. The Princess isn't ready to fly the nest. Whether she chooses Papa or Boyfriend, someone's heart will be broken. But isn't it a Princess's job to break hearts? She has a brilliant plan whereby everyone wins.

Boyfriend is a wannabe Lancelot, out to prove himself. He has grandiose ambitions of chivalric feats to bring him glory at court. Though he goes along with the plan to cheat the test, in the end his pride persuades him that it's better to die than act dishonourably.

The only sensible one is the potion-brewing Auntie. In fairy-tales, motherless heroines are aided by fairy godmothers. This one is a human godmother, an old woman with thirty years experience as a healer, living at the very heart of new medical research and education. But even her wisdom is no match for the bungling of the other characters.

Marie's detailed description of Pîtres, in Normandy, suggests that she knew the place intimately, perhaps from childhood. The town is near Rouen, in the flood plain of a large bend in the river Seine, about 15 metres above sea level. Above it rises a majestic hill, about 120 metres, 400 feet high. The town's website refers to '*un lai de Marie de France, délicate poétesse des années 1100*'.

Against my will, I'm charmed by that phrase *délicate poétesse* to describe Marie. Such perceptions of her have hung around her work like a lavender bag, and vitiated our critical response for more than a century. To think of Marie in faded tapestry colours slights her, and robs the reader of much pleasure in her work. Marie's transparent style can be so deceptive. How does one interpret this apparently simple folk-tale?

It's possible to read it absolutely straight, as a heart-rending tragedy of young love. Or you may look at this condensed epic and see a parody so brilliantly convincing that its irony almost escapes you. Both interpretations are valid. Great tragic dramas include comic scenes, and there's no reason why a clever spoof shouldn't have genuine pathos. I'm sure Marie's playing one mood off against the other.

But a translator needs to choose a tone and stick with it. My solution is to camp it up. The text gives licence to play with rhyme and create witchy spells. Marie's description of the magic potion resembles the patter of a snake-oil salesman. There's a nice cauldron-stirring rhythm, heightened by the repeated negatives, *ne* and *neïs*.

> *Par mescines l'ad esforcié,*
> *Un tel beivre li ad baillié,*
> *Ja ne serat tant travaillez*
> *Ne si ateint ne si chargiez,*
> *Ne li resfreschist tut le cors,*
> *Neïs les vaines ne les os,*
> *E qu'il nen ait tute vertu,*
> *Si tost cum il l'avra beü.*

> However weakened by exhaustion
> Bowed down by burdens or affliction
> Depressed in spirits by emotion
> And the anguish of the soul –
> This medicine will make him whole.
> By the powers of cabbalism
> It restores the organism
> Acting through the venous system
> From the beating of the heart
> It circulates to every part
> Right to the marrow of the bones!
> Here's an end to sighs and moans.

The school at Salerno is of the greatest importance in the history of medicine, and is considered to be the forerunner of modern universities. It was founded around the year 800, in a Benedictine monastery, and was a thriving institution by the 11th century. There was peaceful, untrammelled interchange of knowledge from the Greek, Jewish, Arab and Christian traditions. New ideas developed through this cross-fertilization. Furthermore, Salerno was famous for the education of women healers, people who in later times might have been persecuted as witches.

The most famous of these women, if only in legend, was Trotula, who is mentioned in Chaucer's *Wife of Bath's Tale*. Trotula is still the subject of debate about her status, sex, contribution to science, even her very existence. What is certain is that around 1100 AD, someone using that name wrote a pioneering treatise on midwifery.

Though Marie doesn't cite Trotula by name, my hunch is that Auntie is a fictional portrait of her. Whether she was a real person, a scholar's pseudonym, or a cant name for a cunning-woman or old wife, is irrelevant here. In Marie's day, people believed in her. Trotula's medical texts would have come to the attention of women of learning, whether they were scholarly nuns or wives in charge of great households. They include recipes for cosmetics, such as courtly ladies might use. Marie de France has a wide range of reference, and is well versed in current ideas. She would not lightly pass up an opportunity like this.

Délicate poétesse just sounds better, more concise, in French. To describe Marie, our English *mots justes* would have to include refined, fastidious, subtle, sensitive. God help anyone who ever dares to call me a delicate poetess!

VII : YONEC

I've already mentioned the theory that Marie de France may have been the Abbess of Shaftesbury. But I'm even more interested in another hypothesis, identifying her as Marie de Meulan, daughter of a prominent Norman family. This Marie had children, and her care for them may be reflected in some of the stories. She was married to Hugh Talbot, baron of Cleuville, whose extensive estates in southern England included land in Herefordshire and Gloucestershire. These counties border on Monmouthshire, in South Wales, where *Yonec* takes place.

Great Norman families were peripatetic. According to the seasons and their whim, they would move, with their retinue, from house to house across their lands. They'd spend a period of time in each place, until they got bored or supplies ran out. This arrangement allowed time for each household to recover from one onslaught and prepare itself for the next. They would also pay formal visits, lasting days or weeks, to neighbouring lords, to hunt, feast, plan marriages, catch up on news and generally socialise.

In *Yonec* and *Milun*, Marie de France clearly describes the landscape of South-east Wales. Maybe she knew the area from experience. Perhaps that's how she learned these two marvellous stories. Whatever went on at the political and military end, ordinary people would have rubbed along together well enough. The fields still needed tending. I like to think that Marie might have listened attentively to a Welsh storyteller, and discussed the art with him/her. She could not have written the *Lais* if she weren't good listener. The Plantagenet kings dealt harshly with Wales, yet this story is a harmonious fusion of Anglo-Norman and Celtic themes.

Despite its solemnity and tragic end, *Yonec* is my favourite of the twelve lais. I love its sense of mystery, which seems to reach back to time immemorial. The central motif of the bird impaled in a trap appears in folk-tales from several nations. But this is a Celtic story – the names Yonec and Muldumarec are evidence of that. It might possibly be significant that the Welsh name for Gawain, originally Arthur's most perfect knight, is Gwalchmai, which means Hawk of May.

There are clear associations between *Yonec* and the Middle English *Corpus Christi Carol*, which is as lovely as *Yonec*, and even more enigmatic. It comes from the same deep part of the psyche. The earliest known text of the carol is of 16th century date, but the song may well be earlier, and taken from the oral tradition.

Just as in the carol, Marie has chosen the wounded and dying hawk as an emblem of Christ's body. The shape-shifting prince takes the Eucharist to establish his religious credentials, and prove that he's neither a spirit nor a satanic creature. He's still in command of his pagan magic, even though he has adopted the Christian faith.

My instincts about *Yonec* go far back in time. Countless religions and cults centre on blood sacrifice to ensure fertility and prosperity. In Egyptian myth, Isis gathers up and reanimates the dismembered body of her consort Osiris. To ensure a good harvest, John Barleycorn must die and be reborn each year. The Fisher King, made impotent by his perpetually bleeding wound, may only be healed by the Grail. Arthur, slain in battle, lies sleeping in a green hill until he is called to rise again in time of need.

Christ's crucifixion and resurrection subsumed many such magic stories, just as churches were built on ancient sites. The Lady follows the trail of blood along a road, comes to a green hill, finds a door and runs straight through the hill to the other side. This is like a dream vision. In the Christian tradition, the hill is Calvary and the doorway leads to a tomb. In British folk-lore, green hills are gateways to Elfland. To archaeologists, they are barrow mounds where, in antiquity, people buried the bodies and ashes of their dead. In stories, one motif may carry many layers of significance. The green hill is a threshold into the Otherworld, whether it be paradise, dreamland or the domain of the ancestors.

Why is Marie so particular about locating *Yonec* in South Wales, at Caerwent? Caerwent is 10 metres above sea-level, in the plain of the Severn and Wye estuaries. This landscape has supported human communities for more than 7,000 years. The marshes yielded abundant fish, shellfish, wild-fowl and game; the navigable inlets and tributaries made fine trading places. This rich land gave prominence to whoever commanded it.

The area later became associated with the legends of King Arthur. In Marie's day, Norman lords and wealthy religious orders were beginning to build magnificent castles and monasteries across this landscape, stamping their authority on the Welsh Marches, just as the Romans did. There are at least five Norman castles, mostly ruinous, within a six-mile radius of Caerwent. Whether these imposing buildings were military or religious, they must have had the same effect of awe and power on the local population.

I took myself and the OS map to Caerwent for a day of fieldwork and solitary walking. The results astounded me. Further investigation is needed, but in a few hours I found everything I was looking for and more. There's probably enough for a short research paper. Here are my discoveries:

a: In recent centuries, the salt marshes have silted up, or been drained for pasture. But Caerwent was a major market place, and needed good transport. I met an archaeologist who is researching evidence of a navigable river at Caerwent, just as Marie describes the river Düelas where … *in those days, large ships could pass – But no-one now knows where it was.* Each of us felt that our work was partially validated by the other.

b: I made my way to at least one ancient site which, though damaged, meets the criteria of a processional way leading to a ritual site. It's probably one of several in that area.

c: There is a place dedicated to a saint named Aron, which lies on the way from Caerwent to a Norman abbey.

d: One of the 12th century castles near Caerwent belonged to a family whose heraldic blazon is connected with falconry.

e: From the Gwent escarpment, I looked across the Severn and Wye estuaries. It was easy to imagine the bright unweathered stone towers of new castles and churches glinting in such a light, and to see the silver city from the green hill. What a great place to ride a horse and fly a hawk.

This isn't scientific evidence, nor is it a game based on some arcane code. But taken together these observations are suggestive of a story which belongs to this particular place and time.

VIII : L'AÜSTIC

Lovers lie down with the nightingale and rise reluctantly to the song of the lark (see *Romeo and Juliet*, act III scene V). In Breton, nightingale is *éostik* , which Marie transcribes phonetically, adding the French definite article. In Kernewek (Cornish) the bird is *eos*.

Nightingales are summer visitors to the Mediterranean countries, southern Britain and most of Europe. This drab little bird is seldom seen, as it has a habit of skulking in the undergrowth. Yet there's nothing modest about it; that voice carries a long way. The song, with its infinite invention and variation, captivates the human heart like no other.

The lady in *L'Aüstic* says "The world is empty of pleasure if one cannot hear the nightingale sing." How can something so rich and powerful come from such a tiny creature? The nightingale carries heavy literary symbolism on its frail shoulders. The song is intense, melancholy, and its season is short; music that says everything about beauty, passion and the brevity of youth. It's a metaphor for love, desire, lasciviousness; something sublime and at the same time, wanton. It is therefore dangerous. You can't listen to the nightingale, or fall in love, without wonder and thankfulness. Yet killjoys would say that worship belongs to God alone.

L'Aüstic is poised between tragedy and sentiment, pathos and bathos. Many have read this as a poignant tear-jerker. I think Marie is dancing from one mood to another, with satirical results. Polonius would call my version a tragical-comical-historical-pastoral. The husband's dispatch of the nightingale is a moment of madness and horror. The swine is cruel to animals and heartless to his wife. It's easy to imagine a storyteller grimacing wildly, and using his hands to mime the neck-wringing.

As counterpoint to Aüstic's sad fate, there's something ridiculously over the top about the grieving knight, who travels the world clutching his bird-reliquary. From the first, we know that the lady is a silly woman – she chooses him because he's an insistent suitor and has a flashy reputation. Best of all, he's handily placed next door, where she can keep an eye on him. She just loves to be adored. Their irresponsible grand passion adds up to no more than the baubles they toss to one another.

This is a clear case of *démesure*. True lovers, like Tristan and Iseult, would have scaled that garden wall and eloped long ago, whatever the risk. These two are playing at it, and trap themselves in their own game. The innocent nightingale is the scapegoat for their folly. Is this a metaphor? Perhaps the strangled bird is a coded way of saying that the lover is murdered or mutilated by the jealous husband.

The killing of the bird is a pitiful moment, and I'm sure Marie's readers and audiences would have shed a tender tear. But this was an age when lark pie was a delicacy and small birds were eaten as a matter of course. I think we're supposed to laugh at our sentiments, and ask : Where is the sense of proportion? And there is none, except in Marie's deft telling, and in our responses to the questions posed by this fond tale.

Here are the final verses of a traditional song I learnt at primary school. The tune is a beauty to sing. I'd forgotten that *The Sweet Nightingale* is from Cornwall, until I heard it sung by local musicians. In the English text, *fond* has the connotations of both tender and foolish, but I don't know if this double meaning is the same in Cornish. I was only nine when I learnt it, so the connotations of those valleys below were lost on me.

The Sweet Nightingale

... So she sat herself down
With him on the ground

267

On the bank where the primroses grow
And she heard the fond tale
Of the sweet nightingale
    As she sings in the valley below. (repeat refrain)

The couple agreed
To be married with speed
And along to the church they did go
Now no more she's afraid
For to walk in the shade
    Or to sit in those valleys below.

An Eos Hweg (Eos = nightingale, hweg = sweet, delightful).

... Eseth dhymmo, sur,
Genev vi yn lur,
Yn mysk an brialli y'n lan.
An lev ty a glyw
A-woeles y'n sklyw,
    A'n eos y'n nansow a gan

Akordys yns i
A dhemedhy devri,
Ha dystowgh dhe'n eglos dhe vos.
Namoy hi ny skon
Dhe gemeres y dhorn
    Ha kerdhes y'n nans ryb an koes!

IX : MILUN

Milun has a strange gear-change in the middle. The first half is the engaging tale of the soldier, his lady, their infant son, the jealous husband and the go-between swan. Then suddenly, twenty years whizz by. Tender scenes and lovers' schemes turn into a ripping yarn about jousting and the quest for renown. This narrative disjunction is finally resolved when father and son discover one another, and the lovers are united at last.

Mediaeval romances proceed episodically: the protagonist endures perilous trials, sees marvels, has fateful encounters, until the revelation at journey's end. *Guigemar, Lanval, Le Fresne* and *Yonec* follow this form. These stories are tied up with no threads left dangling. But the change of tone in *Milun* grates on my ear. Fractured harmony might be ignored in other writers, but Marie de France is noted for her precise, lucid, elegant phrasing. There has to be a reason for the eccentric structure of *Milun*.

The first section concerns emotion and intimacy, the second is about action and glory – the feminine and masculine aspects of the psyche. Both journeys may lead to danger, whether it's to be imprisoned by your cruel husband, or to get knocked off your horse by a charging maniac in full armour.

Milun is the third and last of the lais in which the central emblem is a bird, symbolising the essence of a love relationship. The intriguing motif of the swan-messenger grabs our attention. This device focuses the suspense on the feminine side of the story, the two lovers.

Will their affair be discovered? What will happen when the lady's husband finds she's not a virgin? Who will care for the baby boy? Can there be a happy ending?

After a twenty-year interval, the emphasis shifts to the fortunes of the young man and his father. Their priorities are masculine in the extreme. Before they set out to find each other, they must first establish their position in the chivalric pecking order. Ostensibly it's a matter of pride; neither man wants to let the other down. But it's also an evasive tactic to delay the emotional shock of discovery and reunion.

The son says "I must live up to my father's illustrious reputation. I'll go abroad and prove myself the worthiest, most valorous of knights." When this is accomplished, he'll set off to look for his parents. His sense of identity lies in his military career, and his long-lost family comes a distant second. Milun says: "This new knight is the talk of Europe. He's even eclipsing my image. He needs to be taught a lesson. I'll seek him out and face him in a fair fight. Then, when my fame's established beyond doubt, I'll go on a quest to find my son." As a professional knight, both his self-worth and his livelihood depend on physical strength, skill and agility. Aging diminishes him. How will he appear to his only son?

A male swan is called a cob, a female is a pen. In folklore, they represent fidelity, purity, grace and beauty. Sometimes they are the transfigured spirits of children trapped by an evil spell. On the water, and in flight, swans are perfection, free and at ease. But a swan on land, or gathering speed to take off from the water, is an ungainly creature.

Milun and his lady are paired faithfully for life, just as swans are. She's young and very feminine; before even meeting Milun, the girl is dazzled by his reputation. When she finds herself pregnant, she's briefly overcome. But she has the survival instincts of a wild bird, and is sensible enough to devise a plan to safeguard the baby, as well as saving Milun and herself. Later, when her father arranges the marriage, she knows there'll be hell to pay. Alone, she can see no way out but death. Her resourcefulness and fortitude depend on her love for Milun and the child.

The chivalric hero Milun is a knight for hire, which suggests he's had little time for the gentler social skills. Once Milun is tied to marriage, fatherhood and the business of maintaining an estate, will he turn out to be as clumsy as a grounded swan? When he hears of the lady's marriage and captivity, Milun is desolate, but he bounces back when he finds out she's living nearby. He can do what he's best at, devising a cunning plan.

The gizmo is a carrier-swan. His scheme depends on the loyalty of courier and bird. It's brilliant, witty, bonkers, totally unworkable. And it all goes like clockwork. We're in story-land.

In Norman Britain, roast swan was an extravagant dish for splendid feasts. Kings, noble families and monastic houses retained swans in half-captivity, managing the breeding flocks in lakes and rivers on their land. Marie would have been familiar with swanneries. Relics of this custom still continue. Feeding the crowds of birds is a spectacular sight.

Milun offers a wealth of performance opportunities. The text is blasé about the courier delivering the swan to the castle, but the more you think about it, the more absurd his task becomes. It has to be a joke. The journey takes him several miles into hostile territory, and toting the swan would be a pretty conspicuous business. How do you carry a resentful bird measuring 152cm (5 feet) from beak to tail? An adult weighs around 15 kilos (33lbs). A captive bird would be even fatter.

A jongleur might turn his forearm into a swan's neck, elaborating the mime by wearing a white sleeve and painting a pair of beady eyes on his hand. Imagine the outraged bird wrinkling his beak into a sneer and aiming hefty pecks at the servant's nose, eyes and crotch. When (in my version, not Marie's) the courier bribes the castle gate-keeper, I picture the puppet swan picking coins one by one from his hand, and doling them out to the porter.

Since he's trusted by Milun, the courier is either his subaltern or personal servant, trained in a grand Anglo-Norman household. Such a man would have courtly manners and more than a touch of arrogance. He'd stick out like a sore thumb among the South Walians, and must rely on his wits to get through the journey without causing a scene. So I've re-invented his dialogue with the castle porter, and made it a mini-drama.

Like *Yonec*, Milun is set around the great Roman legionary town of Caerleon-on-Usk. On my visit to South Wales, I was seeking clues to the origins of *Yonec* and *Milun*. Ten miles east of Caerleon, three miles south of Caerwent, stands the magnificent Caldicot Castle (not to be confused with Caldicot Manor in Kevin Crossley-Holland's *Arthur Trilogy*). The castle is on an ancient site commanding a wide view of shipping on the Severn Estuary. Caldicot stands by the road and the Neddern river which would have carried goods to the market at Caerwent (Venta Silurum).

In 1158, Humphrey de Bohun, Earl of Hereford, became lord of the manor. The keep and curtain walls of the present castle date from his time, which is spot on for Marie de France. When I saw the modern banner on the door of Caldicot Castle, I was astonished. The emblem of the de Bohun family is a swan, wearing a crown-shaped collar and a chain. It comes from the chivalric legend of the Swan-Knight. Swans are fairly common in heraldry, but even so, the de Bohuns were at the top of the tree. Taken together with my discovery of another castle with a falconry badge *(Yonec)*, I find this swan significant. Did Marie intentionally include references to powerful Norman families in South Wales?

X : CHAITIVEL

I used to hate *Chaitivel*. It's not an uncommon reaction. At first reading this is a miserable story of protracted agony, gratuitous violence and – absolutely explicitly – no sex. Why would anyone want the hassle of translating it? As a problem piece, it ranks with *Equitan*, a biter-bit story with a nasty end for the villains. *Chaitivel* is a straight-faced parody of a courtly love tragedy, whereas *Equitan* is a sort of dirt-free neutered fabliau.

Unless you are a mediaevalist, it takes a while to get the point of the satire, which Marie delicately hints at. 12th century readers, steeped in allegory and the Seven Deadly Sins, would have been alert to the lady's emotionalism and egomaniac vanity. In our terms, she's a pampered air-head. Modern readers may need clues to her folly, if they're not to be overwhelmed by this grim and gruesome story.

It goes on and on about jousting until you wonder why you're bothering to read it. Then pow, she hits you right between the eyes. The run-up is seemingly going nowhere at tedious length. Mediaeval readers were used to this stuff, but surely ladies must have been fed up with endless boastful anecdotes at dinner. Could this be Marie's send-up of a jousting bore?

Marie's knock-out punch doesn't come until 195 of 240 lines of almost unrelenting CHAAARGE-bang-crash chivalry. This two-dimensional world, illuminated in heraldic colours, reminds me of the dream games in *Alice Through the Looking-Glass*.

The lady who had great good sense
is unnamed, as are all the characters in this tale. We know nothing about her apart from the conventional list of accomplishments. There's no mention of husband, family, parents, servants or household. She exists in the abstract, with no other persons to influence her behaviour. Of the leading female characters in the *Lais*, she's the one who has perfect independence and freedom of choice. And what use does she make of it?

She sits, in her beauty and courtliness, watching the mêlée from her vantage in a turret. She has all the warmth and grace of the queen on a chessboard, or in a pack of cards. This is a contest between manipulative Venus and action-man Mars. For the lady, everything that unfolds on the field below is part of a drama in which she is the heroine. Her ambition is not to form a relationship with a man, but to be the object of worship. Even after the tragedy, she learns nothing. She plans grandiose funeral arrangements which focus on her own spurious grief. What other woman has been adored by four such paragons, and caused them great anguish? Then she discovers her new calling in life – she's an Artist, and tomorrow she'll compose a lai about Her Four Sorrows, *Les Quatre Dols*. This poem will immortalise the soulful tragedy. Why, anyone can write a masterpiece in rhymed tetrameters!

This would be an apt point for Marie to sign her work, and propose the enduring quality of her own writing, as opposed to ephemeral dross produced by sentimental amateurs. The implication is there, and Marie doesn't feel the need to make it clearer by invoking her name. So I do it for her. Let this be a triumph of Marie over the third-rate Anon.

The four champions

are her pawns, un-named, undifferentiated. As dedicated fighting men, their time would have been spent acquiring and perfecting the protocol and skills of a knight, such as dexterity with arms, horsemanship, courtly manners, strength, battlefield tactics, command. Unlike the lady's elaborately recorded virtues, we can take at face value the assertion that they are young, talented and gorgeous:

> Although but lately come of age, / In their brief time upon the stage / They were outstanding, cut a dash / Gleaming from spurs to sabretache; / Generous, valiant, never flash, / Each one a regular El Cid – / They handsome were, and handsome did.

There's no description of wisdom and intellectual abilities to match those of the lady who had great good sense. It's pathetically easy to convince each of them that he's her one-and-only. They are willing lapdogs, imagining her brief attention is genuine reciprocity, just as she deludes herself that encouraging a schoolboy crush is true love.

Contrary to the Hollywood image, jousting was not the central sport at a tourney. The big event was the mêlée, a pitched battle between opposing camps. It would begin as an artificial rivalry rather than a grudge match. Sometimes the teams would be decided by where they set up their tents. I would call this a mock battle, except that in the 12th century they used real weapons, swords, spears, axes, maces. As anger rose, a mêlée might quickly turn to carnage, as it does in *Chaitivel*.

In literature, ladies find the spectacle arousing; each has favourites to cheer on. But how much bloodshed can one witness before revulsion sets in? If not disgust, then tedium. Surely a lover, wife or mother would feel that the glory in such a death was nothing but fool's gold. In *Chaitivel*, the lady eggs on her champions with the emotional depth and sincerity of a pompom-twirling cheerleader. Poor boys.

In 1130, Pope Innocent II attempted to ban tournaments. Killing in sport could scarcely be defined as holy war. His edict even forbade Christian burial to those who died in the fights. Note that the lady ostentatiously ignores this proscription. Henry II of England also tried to proscribe tourneys, for reasons of good government. Knights going home from a mêlée were prone to criminality. These were tough guys in the pay of powerful men, and the last thing Henry wanted was a country racked by private wars between rival barons.

These bans proved unpopular and unworkable. Imagine a world-wide law against football. Church and monarchy were in a cleft stick; neither had a standing army, yet neither wanted the peace to be shattered by random outbreaks of mayhem. Kings and Popes deemed it necessary to have a pool of great landowners able to provide trained, fully armed soldiers at need. The Church wanted men to fight in futile crusades. The Plantagenet kings had little fear of an invasion of the British Isles, but they needed armies to defend their estates in France, which they valued above all else.

Love and glory make a heady mix. But the combination of adrenalin, testosterone and frustration is deadly dangerous. Our knights are sexually frustrated and have to wait for the safety valve of a fight to let off steam. The delay before the start of the tourney at Nantes causes unrest and hooliganism. A pall of animosity is in the air at the opening ceremony. The young men ride out in splendour, to meet their death. All but one.

The maimed knight

Chaitivel, for obvious reasons, makes big strong men turn a funny colour. The poem pulls no punches and doesn't sanitise violence. Thigh wounds in mediaeval literature often signify castration. Marie suggests rather than states the consequences and extent of the knight's ghastly injury. I've made it explicit. In reality, it would have been almost miraculous to survive the shock, blood-loss and subsequent infection of such a wound.

The knight's partial recovery seems like a personality change. It gives him an identity, so the reader can empathise with him as with no other figure in the story. Before his wound, he's introduced as a dashing young chevalier, then a deluded love-sick youth, then a war-mad soldier-boy recklessly riding into danger.

On his sick-bed, he develops wisdom, philosophy, tact and gentleness beyond his years. The lady's selfish folly is all too clear when she announces her poetry project. Yet he doesn't rebuke her or show anger. Patiently, he debates with her, posing one of the great questions : Can death be worse than hopeless, helpless suffering? When she agrees to change the name of her poem, we could almost believe that she's learned a lesson from him. But no, she's just agreeing with him, so we can all admire her kindness. And when all's said and done, *Chaitivel* really is a nicer, more intellectual-sounding title.

The word *chaitivel* is difficult, with connotations of falling, captivity, abjection – in Shakespearean terms, a caitiff. Other translators render it as The Unhappy One, The Dolorous Knight, The Wretch. My title, Sir Wanhope, though archaic, isn't a cliché. This is one of those Anglo-Saxon words that should never have fallen from use. Its sonorous tone carries the full weight of despair.

I've added nuances to the dialogue, while trying to retain the solemn, melancholy tone of the voices. It seems to me vital that the wounded knight should retain his wisdom and dignity. I've given him an archaic vocabulary, with artfully placed quotations from the Bible, John Donne and *Moby Dick*. The narrative is larded with faux mediaevalisms, in the hope that readers will spot my intentional irony, rather than run screaming.

In a sense, even after the debate, this remains the lady's story, the tragedy of her cold and loveless heart. She is more *chaitivel* than he. But because she's utterly unfeeling, she'll never experience wanhope, or comprehend the pity and sadness evoked by her fable. She doesn't even know what's missing from her soul. Her maimed knight may yet find the strength to move on, but for her, there's no hope.

Other commentators point out that the last three lines have four repeats of a negative phrase:

> *Ici finist, il n'i ad plus;*
> *Plus n'en oï, ne plus n'en sai,*

Ne plus ne vus en cunterai.

It ends here, there is no more. No more I heard, no more I know. I will tell you no more.

XI CHEVREFOIL

Tristan & Iseult is the most haunting of love stories. It pervades the music, literature and art of the Middle Ages. Marie expects her aristocratic audience to be familiar with the story. The earliest extant texts are in French, dating from the mid-late 12th century. Yet *Tristan* is older; a Celtic legend from the oral tradition, Cornwall's great cultural gift to the world. Many, me included, believe there's a grain of truth in it. I have little space to tell it.

Iseult of Ireland is to marry King Mark of Cornwall; the royal pair have never met. By mishap, the young bride and Tristan, Mark's son, drink a love-potion intended for the wedding night. Thenceforward, they live for one another. Try as they will, self-restraint is intolerable. Their lives become a pattern of farewells, passionate meetings, betrayal, discovery, exile. More than once, they narrowly escape trial and execution. Eventually, Tristan goes into exile in Brittany, where he marries Iseult White Hands. The marriage is unconsummated. One day, Tristan is gravely wounded in a fight. A ship is sent to ask Iseult to heal him; the signal is to be white sails if she is coming, black sails if she refuses. White Hands, in her jealousy, tells Tristan that the sails are black. His heart breaks. Iseult arrives to hear cries of grief throughout the town. She is too late. Arriving at his deathbed, she lies beside Tristan's body, embraces him and dies in a wild rapture. Now, whether in heaven or hell, they may never more be parted. The lovers are buried side-by-side; on each grave grows a plant, and the two intertwine.

The fleeting episode of the hazel-tree and the honeysuckle occurs only in Marie de France. In this miniature she distils one golden moment snatched from the misery of separation. It epitomises the whole. From the outset, we know it will end in tragedy.

Tristan's music

If a translation of *Chevrefoil* doesn't sing, it has failed. In this lai above all, the poetry must come first; if it can't be rendered literally in verse, then it should be recreated, re-enacted. Tristan is a poet, bard and musician – a Celtic Orpheus who can break hearts and sing the birds down from the trees. Tristan poems therefore present a challenge to translators, as if the man himself threw down the gauntlet, saying "Beat that!".

At first, I planned to choose a poetic form that would differentiate *Chevrefoil* from the rest of the collection. I tried an imitation of *Sir Gawain and the Green Knight* but alliteration, with its strong stresses and obsessive repeated sounds proved to be too masculine and unsubtle for the delicacy of this poem. Back to the drawing board.

Pentameters aren't deft enough for Marie. Tetrameters, so concise in English, need to be supple to carry such elliptical meaning and condensed emotion. Free verse lacks the metrical music to hold it together. So rhyme it must, which poses a problem:

> Pity translators. There are fuck all
> Rhymes for the English Honeysuckle.
> Some pounce, with obvious relief,
> Upon the literal Goatleaf .
> Far more euphonious, I find
> Are sweet Woodbine, or Withywind.

It was time to walk and talk to trees. Grigson's *An Englishman's Flora* is a great resource for plant-lore and regional names, but honeysuckle has few dialect variations. Woodbine is most common; it appears in *Midsummer Night's Dream*. But I rejected the name, as it has unwanted associations with the tobacco industry. In parts of England, withywind is bindweed, convolvulus. But happily, in Devon, this lovely word means honeysuckle.

Further inspiration came from the Border Ballads. Elaborate poetic form wasn't needed. Folk-songs are held together by simple refrains, just as the plants intertwine:

The young tree in the green wood / Sweet honey in the flower.

Hazel and honeysuckle

are useful plants, thriving in hedgerows and coppices. Tristan goes to poor peasants for news and a bed for the night. Coppiced woods, often centuries old, would have been part of their village economy. Cob-nuts yielded food and oil. Hazel coppice gave stakes and stems for hedging, wattle-and-daub, hurdles and thatching spars. Pigs foraged through the undergrowth, manuring the soil and providing pork and ham for winter. Hazel was turned into charcoal which, in Mark's Cornwall, would be needed for smelting tin.

In the still-rooms of great mediaeval houses, honeysuckle flowers were dried as a sweet strewing herb, distilled for perfumes and used to concoct a cough-remedy. But to Marie de France, honeysuckle would have been most familiar as a delightful garden plant, trained around arbours and twining in the hedges of garden walks. The flowers are pollinated by moths, so the fragrance is at its headiest after dusk. For lovers in the garden at night, the scent of honeysuckle had the same effect as the nightingale's song.

These plants are blatantly sexy. They burst into spring green, flaunt catkins with abundant clouds of pollen, waft the scent of their throaty flowers. In literature, the honeysuckle's long petals are likened to lady's fingers, and are so named in some regional dialects. But I think it's facile to assume that Marie's image points to the honeysuckle as the delicate little woman clinging to the strong upright male. This is true in over-romantic Victorian symbolism, where the twining "female" plant is usually ivy, as may be seen in costume jewellery. But tales of Tristan and Iseult are robust. The two are self-reliant adults, not co-dependents. And they are indivisible lovers unto death.

Honeysuckle is not a parasite but an epiphyte. It needs a support, but doesn't rob or consume its host. It is usually seen while in vigorous growth, when the long runners are still tender, groping for young stems to twine around. But once settled in place, the adult plants have strong woody stems; the tight coils constrict the tree so that its trunk grows contorted. Eventually host and honeysuckle are plied together like rope (that's how twisted walking sticks are formed). You can unwind soft-stemmed climbers, but you'd tear your hands to pieces trying to separate hazel and honeysuckle. The only way to do it would be to hack at it with a blade.

Woodsman and wise-woman

Early French versions of the story show Tristan and Iseult as resourceful people versed in the old lore. Tristan is a cunning man in both senses. In the Celtic and courtly traditions he is a huntsman and forester. In one early French text, the lovers make a hide in the woods, living wild for three years on whatever game Tristan and his dog can find and kill. We can assume that Iseult prepared food from roots, herbs and fruit. These were survival skills, not aristocratic pastimes.

Iseult of Ireland first meets Tristan when she concocts medicines to cure him of a deadly wound. Such a skilled healer would get her hands dirty and roughened with honest work. This contrasts with Iseult White Hands, whom Tristan eventually marries. Her soubriquet indicates that she's an aristocratic lady with servants to do things for her, lest she demean herself by toil. Marie's symbol of the honeysuckle might be a reference to Iseult Blanches Mains' pale fingers, to remind us of the betrayal and death that is to come at those white hands.

Since Iseult, like Guinevere, has no children, it occurs to me that both these adulterous queens were wise-women, with the means to prevent conception. It would be a wise and politic choice. If an heir to the throne were of doubtful birth, there would be bloody insurrection, and the queen would be tried for double treason.

Tristan and Mark

In Marie's lai, as in most versions, Tristan is nephew to King Mark of Cornwall. I choose to follow the inscription on the Tristan Stone near Fowey : DRUSTANUS HIC IACIT CUNOMORI FILIUS : Here lies Drustan son of Conomorus (i.e. Tristan son of King Mark).

The passion between the lovers is an unstoppable force of nature, from which there is no escape. If we follow that inscription, then not only is Tristran breaking the chivalric code of honour by cuckolding his liege-lord, he's bringing hurt and shame on his father, whom he loves. If Tristan is Mark's son, then to the mediaeval mind, his intimacy with the Queen transgresses against God. According to church law, Tristan is committing incest with his father's wife – just as Hamlet believes his mother's re-marriage to her dead husband's brother is incest. We are witnesses to a primal struggle in the soul.

In *Chevrefoil*, Iseult is never named in person. She is simply the Queen; a figure of state as well as a woman in love. She's driven to break her bond of duty to Mark of Cornwall, and to her kin in the royal house of Ireland. It was, after all, a dynastic marriage. The tragedy is heightened by the sense of a genuine affection and respect between all three of the participants. There is no villain in this triangle, and the reader's sympathies go out to Mark, as well as to the lovers – though not in equal measure!

The hazel-wand

Tintagel is Mark's castle; not until much later did it become associated with Arthur. But King Mark's residence is at Lancien (Lantyan) near Fowey. Since Iseult's journey goes from there to Tintagel, I imagine Chevrefoil taking place in the lovely setting of the Luxulyan valley. Through the mature woodlands runs an ancient track, once used for transporting goods, including tin. This land-crossing is a link between two harbours, Padstow on the north coast and Fowey on the south, thus avoiding a perilous coastal voyage round Land's End and the Lizard. The trade-route later had a second function as a pilgrim's track. It's now a popular 30-mile footpath, the Saints' Way.

Hazel and honeysuckle had magical properties, averting curses and enchantments. Hazel was particularly powerful, being one of the correct woods for wands and divining rods. Dowsers today still use forked hazel-rods. There's a detail in *Chevrefoil* which puzzles scholars – Tristan's inscription on the hazel-rod. This passage is a garbled rigmarole. Marie states that he writes no more than his name, and yet the Queen reads a great deal more into the message.

We know from other poems that in happier times, Tristan floated sticks down the stream which flowed into Iseult's garden, as a signal to her that it was safe to meet. Some editors suggest that he sent word in advance. Some explain the message as a cryptic, condensed form of writing. Some think he wrote the whole thing – with a knife? But these guys aren't writing poetic versions. Translators must decide what it means in the context of their work.

I've chosen the most emotionally truthful interpretation. Tristan and the Queen surely have that intuitive knowing shared by true lovers: an ability to commune with one another from afar, and at times of need, to sense what is happening in the beloved's heart. Tristan simply writes his name, using the quickly cut notches of the Ogham script, which is found on Celtic inscribed stones. His wand is hazel, a powerful protective wood, and he sets the stick upright in Mother Earth.

XII ELIDUC

Eliduc has splendid set-pieces. In the plan to ambush the besieging army, Marie shows a shrewd grasp of battle-tactics. We'll head them off at the pass! Whether she invented it, read it in a romance, or heard knights talking, that part of the story rings true.

The storm at sea strengthens the belief that "Marie from France" spent part of her adult life in Britain. Imagine how it felt to leave home for an unknown land, in a ship loaded with war-gear. Horses would be supported in belly-slings, to restrain them and prevent them from falling and breaking their legs. In rough weather, people would slide around, the frightened horses would sway in their slings, and the cook's cauldron would boil over. This passage of description could only have been written by someone who knew the abject misery of sea-sickness, and yet retained the strength of mind to observe the sailors at their work. You go green at the gills just reading it:

> *Bon vent eurent e bon oré*
> *E tut le tens aseüré.*
> *Mes quant il durent ariver,*
> *Une turmente eurent en mer,*
> *E un vent devant eus leva*
> *Que luin del hafne les geta;*
> *Lur verge brusa e fendi*
> *E tut lur sigle desrumpi….*
> *Un' hure ariere, un' autre avant,*
> *Issi alouent costeant;*
> *Mut esteient pres de turment.*

They make the crossing with great ease / Till, close to home, the pleasant breeze / Veers suddenly, and with a roar / Drives them at speed away from shore / Far from the shelter of the haven. / Her rudder breaks, her mast is riven / The rigging tangled, mainsail torn, / All hope of rescue seems forlorn…. / For several hours the helpless boat / Miraculously stays afloat. / This way and that, with pitch and yaw, / She's blown about along the shore; / Each moment they may come to grief / On some bleak beach or sunken reef.

The eternal triangle

As I said in my essay on *Guigemar*, we begin the book by riding out of a castle into the spring sunshine. At the end, we walk into an abbey. *Eliduc* evokes subjective responses from readers, according to age, sex and the current state of their love-life. It's the same old story: a happily married man has a mid-life crisis after a set-back at work. His ego bruised, he goes to look for career prospects further afield, leaving his supportive wife to manage things at home. He gets a new job at which he excels; meets a beautiful girl much younger than himself. When she declares her love for him, he's overwhelmed.

The difference is in the conduct of the affair. Guilliadun is so very young. There's something equivocal about their relationship. Unlike the other couples in the lais, they don't consummate their love. This is not making a moral point, but a paper-thin statement about loyalty to liege-lord and wife. In the context of *Le Fresne*, *Yonec* and *Milun*, their love seems ungenerous, less true. Their chastity doesn't make their affair more noble. Responsibility lies with Eliduc, who conceals his marriage from Guilliadun. She's a vulnerable teenager like Juliet, and his deception nearly brings about her death.

Apart from the weasels, it's the autumnal ending of *Eliduc* that lingers in the mind. One can't help but be moved by Guildelüec's dignity and forbearance. How many of us could accept the situation with grace, and resolve it with such generosity? Retreating to a nunnery wouldn't be my choice. Once again, Marie details the founding of a rich abbey. This is a very Norman concept, making an architectural mark on the landscape, and saving one's soul by proxy. Is it a deliberately sour note that Eliduc and Guilliadun enjoy years of conjugal bliss before taking their vows?

Weaselry

Everything in *Eliduc* is true to life until the weasel scene. The surprise is breath-taking, a bold stroke of story-telling, full of sudden movement and colour. But – Why Weasels?

Natural history books debunk oft-recounted rural myths about *mustela nivalis*. Weasels don't suck eggs, or mesmerise their prey. Mediaeval weasel-lore, however, is fascinating. Bestiaries tell us they did indeed have a reputation for healing. It was thought that if by some mishap a baby weasel was killed, its parent knew how to revive it. Note the exactitude of this; it doesn't say 'if the baby died of natural causes' but 'if it's killed by misadventure'. It specifies that parents could restore their offspring to life, but not that any weasel could recover another. The superstition draws on observation. Weasels are diligent mothers; if they're under threat, they carry their babies to safety in their mouths.

This immediately sheds new light on a small linguistic problem that exercises the minds of translators. The Old French for weasel is *musteile*, a feminine noun. The relationship between Ex-Weasel A and Dr. Weasel B can't be deduced: A may be of either sex, and Dr. B could be its mate, or just its friend; as Marie puts it, *sa cumpaine*.

In my translation, I've made A male and Dr. B female, to reflect that Eliduc's wife saves his bacon. But what if Dr. B is A's mummy or daddy? This gives extra subtlety to the story. Marie clearly loved babies; remember the tender descriptions of infant care in *Milun* and *Le Fresne*. If she was indeed Marie de Meulan, wife of Hugh Talbot, she had a family of her own. In this lai there's no overt suggestion that Eliduc and Guildelüec have children. But if they are implied by the weasel episode, then what great sacrifice their mother makes for love of their father. In this light, the story becomes unbearably poignant as she enters the nunnery, leaving them in the care of a young woman they scarcely know.

I still wonder – what human response to weasels makes them healers? Let me speculate. Weasels are long, thin, snake-like animals. Their sinuous bodies enable them to run down the narrow burrows of mice and other small creatures, hence their ability to pop out from a crevice under the altar. In Greek temples, snakes were the protectors of the altar. Both weasel and snake creep through crannies in the ground and fetch back their prey. They could be construed as creatures running at will between earth and the otherworld. Two snakes twine round the wand of Hermes, the caduceus emblem of the medical profession. In mediaeval literature, it would be sacrilege to have a devilish serpent issuing from the altar of a Christian chapel, but a weasel might serve the same symbolic purpose. It comes from below, the land of the ancestors, and runs to the forest to fetch a healing herb. This witchery is sanctified by its holy context in the chapel.

Marie de France was not a naturalist. It's possible that her weasel (and also the animal in the bestiary) is a conflation of several species :- least weasel, weasel, stoat and polecat. The white ermine, symbol of chastity, is the stoat in its winter coat. Weasels change colour too, in areas with cold snowy climates. This could imply a parallel between the animal's whiteness and Guilliadun's virginity.

What of the red flower? Notes to the Penguin translation suggest it might be verbena (officinalis). This is vervain, a famous witch herb credited with magical properties and the ability to cure many ailments and diseases. The plant is scarce in the UK. I've never found one. But judging by photographic illustrations, vervain is an unprepossessing flower of a drab pale pinkish colour. I stick with scarlet pimpernel, which we all know and love. It has far fewer healing uses (snake-bite is one of them). Nevertheless, it looks as though it would put colour in your cheeks. Even if it fails to resuscitate weasels, scarlet pimpernel will tell you the time of day and the weather, and at a pinch, you can use it to save an aristocrat from the guillotine.

Translating *Eliduc*

The longest lai proved the most difficult. In *Chevrefoil*, Marie condenses the Tristan legend into 118 lines. By contrast, *Eliduc* is expansive, with 1184 lines. Like all my versions, this exceeds Marie's in length.

The story has several points of confusion, like all those repetitive sea-crossings. Are we in Brittany now, or Logres? There's a limit to variations on the theme of *So they embark without delay*.

In *Eliduc* there are two kings and at least two messengers, all unnamed. I've developed the character of the chamberlain, so he's become a factotum who acts as courier for both Eliduc and the Princess. He's cheerful, efficient and does it all for love.

RESOURCES

These are the works I've found most helpful. For a comprehensive list, see:
Marie de France : an Analytical Bibliography : Glyn S Burgess (London : Grant & Cutler 1977): Supplement no. 1, 1986; Supplement no. 2, 1997, Supplement no. 3 (Woodbridge: Tamesis), 2007.

Source text

Marie de France : Lais ed. Alfred Ewert (Oxford : Blackwell 1944); re-issued with introduction and bibliography by Glyn S Burgess (Bristol : Bristol Classical Press 1995)

Definitive translation

The Lais of Marie de France trans. Glyn S Burgess & Keith Busby (London : Penguin 1986; 2nd ed. 1999)

Critical study

Marie de France Emanuel J Mickel, Jr. (New York : Twayne 1974)

The Anonymous Marie de France R. Howard Bloch (Chicago: Univ. of Chicago Press 2003)

Other translations

The Lais of Marie de France trans. Robert Hanning & Joan Ferrante (New York : Dutton 1978)

The Ebony Tower John Fowles : includes a translation of *Eliduc* with interesting introductory essay (London : Jonathan Cape 1974)

The Romance of Tristan by Béroul trans. Alan S Fedrick (London : Penguin 1970)

The Lays of Marie de France trans. Eugene Mason (London : Dent 1911)

Natural history

An Englishman's Flora Geoffrey Grigson (London: Phoenix House 1987)

Flora Britannica Richard Mabey (London: Chatto & Windus 1997)

Birds Britannica Mark Cocker & Richard Mabey (London: Chatto & Windus 2005)

MUSIC

Tristan & Iseult The Boston Camerata, cond. Joel Cohen. (450-98482-2 Erato 1989)

Chevrefoil Istanpitta (RVRCD58 Riverrun 2002)

SITES IN SOUTH WALES

Ordnance Survey Map : Explorer OL14 Wye Valley & Forest of Dean.

The Legionary Museum, Caerleon; Caerwent Roman Town; Caldicot Castle, Caldicot.

Biographical Notes

Marie de France is the first named woman poet in the French language. Three works, dating from the late 12th century, are attributed to her. Her *Lais* (short stories in verse) were highly regarded in her day, and they remain an enduring classic. Though little is known of Marie, it's thought that she was raised in Normandy, and spent a significant part of her adult life in Britain.

Jane Tozer spent most of her childhood in Dorset. One rainy day, when she was 8 or 9 years old, she shut herself away with a copy of Coleridge's *Rime of the Ancient Mariner*. Reading it felt like a guilty pleasure, and from that day she was hooked on poetry.

Photo: Maggie Vicuña

She has a degree in English from Cambridge University (New Hall), where she first read the *Lais of Marie de France* as part of an optional paper on the period 1066-1350. In the late 1960s, the only available translation dated from 1911. It was inaccurate and bowdlerized, and written in the phoney-mediaeval style of the Edwardian period. At the age of 20, Jane felt 'Even I could do better than that!' She shelved the project for more than thirty years, but it remained as an ambition.

After graduation, Jane spent a year teaching English in Finland, where she left part of her heart behind. From 1972-1985, she was a curator in museums at Warwick, Glasgow and Manchester, specialising in costume, social history and rural life. In her spare time, she volunteered on archaeological digs, including Colchester and Offa's Dyke. These experiences stimulated an interest in the relationship between landscape and story.

In the summer, Jane works as a part-time castle guide at St. Michael's Mount, where she enjoys storytelling and interpreting history. She lives on a small-holding near Helston with her husband Tony Phillips-Smith, who bears a startling resemblance to her illustrator, Apsley.

Apsley will only say that he is a jobbing artist and cartoonist with an interest in classic cars. He is a volunteer for the National Coastwatch Institution and does odd jobs for Oxfam. He lives in an earthly paradise in West Cornwall with his wife and sundry dogs, cats and chickens. They all think the world of him.